ABOUT THE AUTHOR

Stephen McCormick is Senior Specialist in Business Strategy at the Irish Management Institute (IMI) in Dublin. His earlier career background was in general management, in the private and public sectors. He is the programme leader for the IMI's Business Strategy Diploma and Advanced Management programmes, and he organises customised development for major clients. He consults on strategy development in a wide range of organisations. He has created a successful workshop course for smaller companies which is structured around the workbook part of this volume.

STRATEGY IN ACTION

**A step-by-step guide and workbook,
for small and medium-sized businesses**

Stephen McCormick

Irish Management Institute

BLACKHALL
Publishing

This book was typeset by Artwerk for

Blackhall Publishing,
8 Priory Hall, Stillorgan,
Co. Dublin,
Ireland.
and
Blackhall Publishing,
2025 Hyperion Avenue,
Los Angeles,
CA 90027,
USA.

Email: blackhall@eircom.net
Website: www.blackhallpublishing.com

© Stephen McCormick, 2001

A catalogue record for this book is available from the British Library

ISBN: 1 842180 22 3

Printed in Ireland by
ColourBooks Ltd

CONTENTS

Preface

I wrote this book with the intention of taking some of the mystery out of strategy and making it easy for managers to get to grips with. Much of what is written about strategy makes it appear very complex, but the essence of strategic thinking is very simple, and I have tried to bring that simplicity into these pages, especially in the workbook. Simplicity is in fact the first essential in strategic thinking – it is the capacity to see beyond the confusing detail and discern the shapes of the underlying forces in your company's world.

Strategy is also very practical – it is about the decisions managers must constantly take about how they will use their resources to ensure success in the future. All senior managers are therefore practising strategy, whether with a conscious discipline or not. This book aims to help you do it better.

Strategy in Action will help you to clarify your thinking about where you want to take your business in the years ahead; about what areas of business you want to engage in; and what levels of success you want to aim for. It will help you and your colleagues to develop a clearer sense of long-term purpose.

Having done that, the book will help you to work out how best to achieve your long-term purpose, given your own resources and capabilities, and given the realities of the business environment you live in. It will help you to create a realistic and flexible plan to guide you on your way.

HOW TO USE THE BOOK

The book is in two parts – Part 1 is the Workbook and Part 2 the Reference section.

I recommend that you start by going through the **workbook**. This contains all the basic directions you will need to guide you through the creation of a strategy for your business. In order to keep it as clear and straightforward as possible, I have kept it free of supporting theory and frameworks. You will find that it has a very practical and action-oriented flavour.

As you work through the tasks in the workbook, however, you may occasionally find yourself asking: how do I do that? Are there any tried and tested frameworks or approaches which could be useful here? Is there some background theory which would help me to think more clearly about this issue? The **reference section** contains this supporting material, selected for its relevance to the tasks in the workbook. It is sequenced to parallel the flow of the workbook, and at each stage in the workbook you will find the chapter number for the appropriate reference material.

WHAT THIS BOOK IS NOT

This book is not a textbook. It does not set out to cover all aspects of strategy-making, nor to include all of the many shades of opinion and schools of thought which populate the area. It aims merely to show you a path through the strategy-making task and to light that path with those pieces of theory which I think are most relevant. I believe this is one of those situations where less is more. I wish you well on your journey.

Stephen McCormick
March 2001

Introduction

IS STRATEGIC PLANNING POSSIBLE?

I think it was Mark Twain who said "The art of prophecy is difficult, especially with respect to the future", and prediction has certainly got more difficult in recent times. We all know that life has become very turbulent in high-tech businesses, but many old-economy businesses are now being buffeted – if not actually wiped out – by rapid changes in technologies, markets and industry supply chains.

And so, the argument goes, if we cannot predict accurately how things will be in three or four years' time, how can we sensibly plan that far ahead?

Maybe we can't, and the smartest thing would be to make no plans or commitments, but simply stay flexible, so that we can adapt quickly to whatever emerges. A counter-argument comes from Alvin Toffler, author of *Future Shock* and *The Third Wave*. Toffler's comment is:

> A lot of otherwise very smart people are denigrating strategy today, arguing that it is an obsolete idea. They say that things are changing so rapidly, a company can't really have a strategy; it just needs to be adaptive or agile. This is an attempt to substitute agility for strategy. But if you don't have a strategy and you rely on agility, you will be permanently reactive and will wind up as part of somebody else's strategy.

Very few of us can predict our industry's future with great accuracy more than a year or two ahead. But most of us, if we put our minds to it, could gain an understanding of the main driving forces in our industry, so that we would have a better feel for what was more likely and less likely to develop over the long run. And if we had that understanding, we would be in a better position to plan how we would take advantage of emerging developments and impose our own shape on the future of the industry.

Managers cannot afford the luxury of simply saying "the future is unknowable" and leaving it at that. You have to take decisions today about whether or not to invest in this piece of equipment, to buy this building, to hire these specialised staff. And these decisions require you to have a view about the likely shape of the far future and your company's place in it. You need a methodology to help you to develop that view and update it as you go.

I believe that you can and must manage your future, and this book is designed to help you do it.

Note: Further material on this subject is in Chapter 1 (reference).

Part One

STRATEGY IN ACTION
WORKBOOK AND GUIDE

Introduction to
Strategic Business Planning

"Chance favours the prepared mind."

Louis Pasteur

"Doing things right is important, but doing the right things is critical."

Chester Barnard

Most of us are very busy, and the pressures of everyday business seem to grow endlessly, leaving little time to think about the long term. We don't have much time to speculate on where the world is going, how our industry is changing, and how we might take control of our destiny in the midst of all this. Since we don't spend a lot of time thinking about these things, we may find we are not very confident about our ability to do so.

This workbook is designed to help you to take control of the future direction and development of your business. It will lead you through a simple process which will help you to decide on: the shape of your business; where you want to get to; the problems to be overcome; and how to make the journey, starting from now.

Throughout the workbook, you will find occasional pointers to supporting material in the reference section which may be relevant at that stage.

A Road Map for
Strategic Business Planning

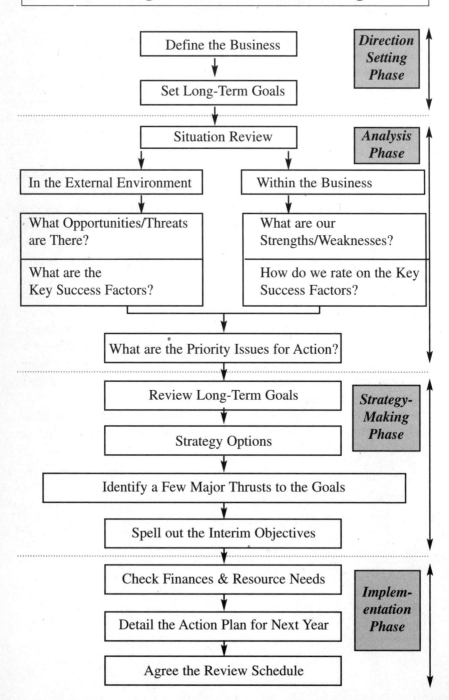

Define the Business

Set Long-Term Goals

Direction Setting Phase

Situation Review

Analysis Phase

In the External Environment

Within the Business

What Opportunities/Threats are There?

What are our Strengths/Weaknesses?

What are the Key Success Factors?

How do we rate on the Key Success Factors?

What are the Priority Issues for Action?

Review Long-Term Goals

Strategy-Making Phase

Strategy Options

Identify a Few Major Thrusts to the Goals

Spell out the Interim Objectives

Check Finances & Resource Needs

Implementation Phase

Detail the Action Plan for Next Year

Agree the Review Schedule

Defining the Business

You can't be the best at doing everything for everybody. As competition intensifies, you need to focus on what you can be best at.

Pareto's Principle says most of your business will come from a relatively small fraction of the total customer base, and from a relatively small fraction of your product range. If you focus closely on the needs of key customer groups, and on excellence in chosen product/service areas, you are likely to build stronger market position.

THREE KEY QUESTIONS:

1. Which **customer** groups/types will I try to serve really well?

2. Which **needs** of those customers could I plan to serve really well? (Do I **know** their needs?)

3. With which **technologies**, **products** or **services**?

Each of these questions has a flip-side. If you are going to focus your efforts on only some of your present base of potential customers, it means giving less attention to the others; you may have to let some of them go. It's a tough decision - none of us likes to let go of anything.

So you should think long and hard as you answer these three questions, and you may need to do a little research in the process. But you **should decide**, and write down explicit answers. You are setting out the strategic shape of your future business.

Note: Further material on this subject is in Chapter 2 (reference).

Business Definition

1. The customer **groups/types** we are primarily aiming at are:

2. We aim to serve primarily the following **needs** of these customers:

3. We will focus primarily on offering these **technologies/ services/products**:

Setting (Provisional) Long-Term Goals

"If you don't know where you're going, you're sure to end up some-where else."

Mark Twain

Setting long-term goals provides a steady strategic direction for the business. It's like navigating by the North Star. In the everyday rough-and-tumble of business life, you can easily get pulled off course by emergencies and short-term opportunities. If you have a clear long-term goal, you never lose sight of where you're heading, and you can quickly pull yourself back on track.

Long-term goals should be set for at least three years out, and up to five years if it seems reasonable to you. At this stage, you should make them ambitious, so that they are attractive and exciting; let yourself dream a little. Ambitious and demanding goals will force you to think much more creatively and boldly about new ways of looking at busi-ness and the needs of customers.

Try to imagine a snapshot of your business as you'd really like it to be in three or five years' time: what is your total revenue/turnover? What profit margin have you? What is your share of your target market? How many staff have you? Where is your office/plant and how big is it? What is your image in your market? What are you notable for? What are you excellent at? What is your personal income?

Write the goal in the present tense. Write it specifically enough that you will know when you have attained it.

Don't be afraid to write this down. Be a little realistic, but do be **ambitious**. If you can't think it, you won't do it.

Note: Further material on this subject is in Chapter 2 (reference).

Setting Long-Term Goals (Continued)

Our goals for the year (   ) are as follows:

1.   Turnover:

2.   Profit margin (or actual profit):

3.

4.

Note: Don't write too many goals. Twenty goals equal no goals. Pick
the few that are really important, and put them in rank order. If
there are a number of principals in the business, you may have to
have a lot of discussion before you can agree all this. It will be
worth the effort.

How are Things Developing?

You have defined the shape of your future business and set out your key long-term goals, so you have a clear view of where you want to get to.

Now you need to form a view of how the world of your business is likely to be changing during that time, and what opportunities and threats this may present. You also need to take a realistic look at yourself and how good you are, to see how ready you are to cope with this future.

First, look at the external environment of the business, and reflect on likely trends over the next few years.

THE ENVIRONMENT

1. Social Changes
   Changing attitudes and values
   Demographic shifts in your market

2. Political/Regulatory Changes
   Trends in legislation
   Trends in public policy

3. Economic Changes
   Growth, inflation, exchange rates, stability, EMU, and so on

4. Technological Changes
   Change in the main technologies used by you and your rivals. Information and communications technologies used by competitors, suppliers and new entrants. How will this affect the structure of the industry?

5. The Competitive Environment

   a. Competitors
   Who are the important ones?
   How strong are they?
   What are their strengths/weaknesses?
   What is their view of the future?
   What are their ambitions and intentions?
   What is their strategy?
   What are their capabilities?
   How will they react to your moves?

b. Customers/Buyers   Market growing? How fast?
                        What alternative products/services are
                        available to customers?
                        Can you bind them in to you more
                        effectively?
                        Who are the most desirable customers?
                        How can you get a strong grip on them?

c. Suppliers   Who are the important ones?
                    '   How is the power balance between you?
                        What are their future intentions?
                        What future binding ties can you create?
                        Can you make them depend on you
                        more than you on them?

Note: Further material on this subject is in Chapter 4 (reference).

Opportunities and Threats

Having considered all of the above, what opportunities can you see which could help you move towards your goals? Try to identify as many as possible, even if they seem a little far-fetched.

Opportunities:

You will also have spotted some possible threats to your business and its proposed development. Identify the main ones you must deal with.

Threats:

Key Success Factors

Can you identify a few key things - maybe two or three, certainly no more than five - which a business such as yours would **absolutely need to have** in order to succeed in this environment?

A good test of Key Success Factors is: if you have all of these, you are about 80 per cent certain to succeed; if you don't have them all, you will most likely fail.

Possession of Key Success Factors is what distinguishes the **winners** in an industry from the also-rans.

Key Success Factors:

1.

2.

3.

4.

Note: *Key Success Factors* may include *resources* (staff, location, information systems, and so on), or *competences* (ability to do certain kinds of business, customer service, and so on), or *link-ages* (with suppliers, intermediaries).

Further material on this subject is in Chapter 4 (reference).
There is also a worked example in Chapter 6 (reference).

Assessing Our Own Firm

Here you take a hard look at yourself, to see how you measure up - in relation to your competitors, and to the opportunities and threats you have identified. Try to look at your firm objectively, as an outsider would, and consider these questions:

1. Performance

How well have you been doing over recent years in relation to:
- Sales/income growth/market share growth?
- Profits/profitability?
- Productivity/cost management?
- Innovation - creating new markets, introducing new services/products?
- Quality and customer responsiveness?

2. Resources

How do you rate your resources:
- Physical (buildings, location, equipment)?
- Human - special skills, technology, and so on?
- Financial - ability to generate capital?
- Market - customer base and image?
- Supplier relationships?
- Distributor/channel relationships?
- Products - range and strength?

3. Capabilities

Do you have, or are you developing, any special capabilities which will distinguish you uniquely in the customer's eyes, giving you a competitive edge?

4. Management and Organisation

Do you have a clear vision of the future? Clear goals and strategy? Are they well communicated to staff? Is there good leadership and motivation? Does the company have a strong and positive culture, oriented to high performance? Is there an appropriate structure? Good supporting systems? Are managers knowledgeable and skilled?

Note: Further material on this subject is in Chapter 5 (reference).

Strengths and Weaknesses

From the above, can you identify some important elements where you feel you are really strong, better than most competitors? List these now as **STRENGTHS**.

Strengths:

Can you pinpoint some areas where you are definitely weak, trailing the main competition? List these as **WEAKNESSES**.

Weaknesses:

A few pages back, you listed a few key factors essential to success in this business. Now that you have looked hard at the resources and capabilities of your firm, ask yourself: how well do we measure up against each of the key success factors? Be critical; pretend you're the bank manager.

Key Success Factors	Comment on how you measure up
1...................................	....
2...................................	....
3...................................	....
4...................................	....
5...................................	....

Does this identify any areas you need to fix in order to succeed?

Areas for attention	Action needed

Priority Strategic Issues

You have now looked at Opportunities, Threats, Strengths & Weaknesses (SWOT Analysis) and you have considered Key Success Factors for your business.

At each of these stages, you may have come across things on which you should act decisively, as they relate to achieving your goals.

1.   You may have spotted one or two really interesting areas of Opportunity which you should exploit.

2.   You may have seen some external Threats against which you had better protect yourself.

3.   You may have noted some competitive Strengths on which you could build.

4.   You may have discovered Weaknesses which leave you exposed and which you should correct.

5.   Wherever an Opportunity lines up with a Strength in the same area, there is a strong case for doing something about it. Wherever an external Threat is matched with an area of Weakness on our part, this is a priority for defensive action.

6.   You may already (on the previous page) have identified some actions you need to take to meet the Key Success Factors you identified.

Each item, from one to six above, is a potential source of **Priority Strategic Issues**, which you should act on if you wish to achieve your goals. Create a list of these, and enter them in the box on the next page.

Priority Strategic Issues and Possible Actions:

Now look at your list. Do a number of the issues or possible actions fit tightly together, so that you could combine them? Do this where you can.

Some of the ideas on your list will seem very important and promising, others more trivial or even doubtful.

Now rank-order your ideas, putting (1) against the most promising and important one, and progressing down through (10) and beyond.

Note: Further material on this subject is in Chapter 3 (reference).
    See Chapter 6 (reference) for a worked example.

Review Long-Term Goals

At the start of this process, you set out your (provisional) long-term goals for the business. They expressed your vision, your ambitions and aspirations for the business.

Then you looked at reality: first in the world outside, the business environment for the next number of years; then you looked at yourself and your resources and capabilities; then you did your SWOT analysis and identified a list of issues and actions which would be important as you push towards your goals.

After all this examination of reality, you should ask yourself: are my goals realistic? Are they over-ambitious and aspirational, pie-in-the-sky? Or are they too conservative, given the interesting possibilities you have discovered? You should now either reaffirm them, or adjust them as appropriate.

Our Firm Goals to the year (   ) are:

1.

2.

3.

Major Strategic Thrusts

On page 17, you set out a list of priority strategic issues and possible actions. You grouped and combined related items, and then you ranked them in order of importance.

What you need to do now is to pick out a very limited number of major thrusts (probably no more than four) which you will pursue as you move towards your goals. Examples of such broad strategic thrusts might be:

*   Build a comprehensive network of distributors;
*   Build outstanding service reputation, supported by excellent customer database and flexible, responsive operations;
*   Build close alliances with selected key suppliers;
*   Introduce major new kinds of business to the portfolio;
*   Enter and dominate a new market area or segment.

If you selected fifteen major thrusts, you will focus on none, and achieve nothing – you will really just drift. So once again, you must take a tough decision and select just a handful, the few you will really give your energy to.

Major Strategic Thrusts:

*

*

*

*

Note: Further material on this subject is in Chapter 3 (reference).
See Chapter 6 (reference) for a worked example.

Interim Objectives

You know your ultimate destination (**Goals**). You know how you plan to get there (**Major Strategic Thrusts**). Now it is important to plan the journey, by setting out the major milestones by which you will mark your progress. You need to identify the interim stages and actions, the stepping-stones which will lead to your goals.

There are two kinds of interim objectives: the first of these is a **milestone** or measure of progress; the second is a **stepping-stone**, a means to the end.

1. **Milestone**: suppose last year's turnover was £2 million, and your forward goal for Year Five is £6 million. Well, it's a nice dream, and it will remain a pipe-dream if you don't pull it closer to you than Year Five. So you should set out interim year-end objectives. Thus, you may conclude that £6 million in Year Five means £5 million in Year Four, £4 million in Year Three, £3 million in Year Two and £2.5 million in Year One – the current year.

   Suddenly your dream has become very explicit and demanding, and you have to start **now** to do things which lead to the goal.

   Planning is not about deciding what you will do in the future; it is about deciding what you must do **now** in order to make the desired future happen.

2. **Stepping-stone**: say you have set yourself a goal of trebling turnover by Year Five, and this will involve increasing staff, some of them specialised in a new service/product area you aim to exploit.

   You need to think your way towards the goal, identifying what extra staff will be needed at various stages. You should consider how long it would take to induct them and get them up to speed; this will take you back to you when you need to recruit them.

EXAMPLE: A MEDIUM-SIZED INSURANCE BROKERAGE IN DUBLIN

Goal: £6 million turnover by Year 5

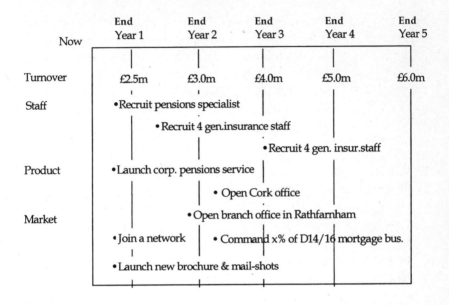

	Now	End Year 1	End Year 2	End Year 3	End Year 4	End Year 5
Turnover		£2.5m	£3.0m	£4.0m	£5.0m	£6.0m
Staff		•Recruit pensions specialist	• Recruit 4 gen.insurance staff		•Recruit 4 gen. insur.staff	
Product		•Launch corp. pensions service	• Open Cork office			
Market		•Join a network •Launch new brochure & mail-shots	• Open branch office in Rathfarnham • Command x% of D14/16 mortgage bus.			

You are really thinking of each goal area as a project, and constructing a project plan to chart your way to it.

Now try to chart your goals and interim objectives on the sheet overleaf (make more copies if necessary).

Year End	Year 1	Year 2	Year 3	Year 4	Year 5
Goal Area					

Check out Finances and Identify Resource Needs

FINANCES

Now it is time to cost your plan. For each year, you need to think through the costs which will be incurred in all parts of the business. These will include:

- New staff – recruitment, salaries, cost of training;
- New equipment and materials;
- Marketing – brochures, advertising, promotion and so on;
- New systems – software, data bases, computer and telecomms;
- Building and overheads.

You must set the costs against expected revenues, then project profits and cash flows – and consider what extra financing, if any, will be needed.

RESOURCES AND ORGANISATION

As you start to finalise your plan, check that you have thought through all the implications, and identified all the necessary changes. Consider the following:

- **Organisation Structure** – should it change? when?
- **Systems** needed: I.T.; communications and so on;
- **Staff** numbers and categories;
- **Staff** skills development needed;
- **Premises and Locations**;
- **Equipment and Facilities**.

Note: Further material on this subjects is in Chapter 7 (reference).

Action Plans

You have thought through your strategies now in detail, and you have identified all the associated resource and organisation changes.

You have planned how you will progress towards your goals via a set of interim objectives which are set out on a time scale.

To get the whole thing moving, you now need an action plan for the first year. This will detail the tasks necessary to achieve the first year's objective; it will specify when they must be done, and by whom.

Create your own Action Planning Sheets, which might take something like the form below:

Objective	Actions Required	Completion Date	By Whom

Note: Further material on this subject is in Chapter 7 (reference).

The Review Schedule

You may start into strategic planning with a great burst of enthusiasm; you may get quite excited by your ambitious goals, and by the new sense of direction and purpose you have created for the business. But be assured, all of this will fade and be submerged by the pressure of everyday operational events and demands. It will all have been a waste of time and energy, **unless** you commit yourself to a formal discipline whereby you **regularly** review how you are progressing against the plan. Some firms do this every month, but the very **minimum** frequency should be three months.

What this means is that you should schedule, in your diary and those of your colleagues, a formal meeting at a **fixed** time to review **strategic** rather than operational progress. You could run it on the same day as one of your regular operational meetings, but do set a separate and fixed time-slot for it.

General Dwight D Eisenhower once said: "*No plan ever survives the first contact with the enemy*". As you move into the future, there will be many unforeseen developments for which your plan has not fully prepared you. Don't worry; this is normal and inevitable. As the world changes, and new information becomes available, you simply adjust your plan accordingly. It is unlikely that your Business Definition or your long-term Goals will have to be modified, but some of the more detailed elements are sure to change a little.

If you are having regular review meetings every few months, this is the ideal opportunity, while measuring progress against the plan, to assess whether the plan needs adjusting and updating. A good plan is a flexible plan.

Part Two

STRATEGY IN ACTION

REFERENCE SECTION

CHAPTERS 1-7

CHAPTER ONE

Introduction to Strategy

What is strategy all about?
Is strategic thinking different from strategic planning?
Can strategy cope with rapid change?
Is there one best way to make strategy?
Are there alternative approaches to
developing strategies?

"Some people make things happen, some watch while others make things happen, and some wonder what happened."

Anonymous

WHAT IS STRATEGY ALL ABOUT?

Strategy: the company's long-term vision of its role, purpose and goals, and the pattern of actions and resource allocations necessary to achieve them.

Strategy is concerned with two broad questions:

1. **What** does the company aspire to achieve over the long term?
2. **How** does it intend to do it?

We can also say that strategy is primarily about shaping the **big picture** and the elements which affect it. Specific and short-term tactics come after that. Strategic decisions tend to be large-scale and hard to reverse. They often involve major commitments, and sometimes a significant change in direction for the company. They may relate to moving into a new market or technology area, entering a different business, or developing a new basis for competing in the market.

If we are to contrast the strategic mindset with the operational mindset, we might say that while *operations* are concerned with *efficiency* (doing things right), *strategy* is concerned with *effectiveness* (doing the right things). To put that another way, we might ask: is it more important to row the boat quicker or to row in the right direction? The ideal, of course, is to do both.

Strategy aims primarily to set out the long-term path of development for the company, to provide consistent direction and orientation. A good strategic plan will spell out how to execute the proposed strategy, while allowing the flexibility to adapt to changing circumstances.

Successful strategies usually contain the following elements:

1. A definition of the Scope or Domain of the company, indicating what business it will and will not be in;
2. A few simple and energising long-term goals;
3. An analysis of the competitive and larger environment;
4. A review of the company's resources and capabilities, and an explicit identification of its proposed source of competitive advantage;
5. A clear outline of how the company intends to shape the elements in 3 and 4 in order to achieve 1 and 2.

IS STRATEGIC THINKING DIFFERENT FROM STRATEGIC PLANNING?

It shouldn't be. To quote Gary Hamel, strategy is about revolution. What he means is that if you are thinking of a future that is pretty much the same as today, you are really just involved in some incremental business planning; and that might be OK if you're in a very stable business environment.

Strategy-making, on the other hand, is concerned with envisaging a somewhat different future (or futures) and with producing a cohesive design for how the company might cope with, or shape, that future in order to prosper. This requires a thinking process that is open and enquiring, imaginative and entrepreneurial.

The outputs of this process are: a strategic vision and business definition for the company; a set of long-term goals and short-term performance targets; and the competitive moves and internal resource developments needed to deliver these. Taken together, these amount to a strategic plan which is based on real strategic thinking. In many best-practice companies, this process will have involved all or most of the management team. The Plan which emerges is a slim document, serving merely as an *aide-memoire*, with action plans and targets for the first year.

The company's business definition and long-term goals, if they are properly thought out, should not need updating for a few years. However, the strategies to achieve them will have to be adjusted as conditions change from year to year. Many of these changes are not fully predictable, and managers need to understand the thrust and logic of the strategy in order to be able to modify it as required. Managers must track changes in technologies, buyer preferences, competitor behaviour and new business models, and adapt the strategy accordingly.

There are still a few companies which continue to suffer from the Strategic Planning blight of the 1970s. In these companies there is a

regular, scheduled annual cycle in which managers and planning special-
ists labour to produce, to a standard format, this year's update of the
Strategic Plan. This is usually a couple of inches thick, in an impressive
cover, and is utterly useless. Why? It is produced as a bureaucratic
routine, there is rarely any original or creative content, it typically
assumes the future is a linear extension of the past, and the long editing
process ensures it is out of date by the time it is circulated. In these
companies Strategic Thinking certainly is different from Strategic
Planning.

CAN STRATEGY COPE WITH RAPID CHANGE?

Much of the business world now changes so fast that it can seem a
waste of time trying to make strategy for the long term. In this turbulent world, the practice of strategy becomes harder all the time; so hard,
in fact, that many companies despair of being able to take any kind of
positive strategic view. They talk, instead, of having an "emergent" or
"incremental" strategy. And maybe they have. But often this is just
management-speak for no strategy at all; what they are really doing is
reacting as flexibly as they can to the opportunities and threats which
their world serves up to them.

It is certainly difficult to predict the future, but perhaps you can try
to shape it. If you are going to shape it, you need to have a point of view
about the key driving forces of that future; about what will constitute
customer value in a range of plausible futures; and what kinds of business systems will have the best hope of creating and delivering the new
value.

The strategy you select needs to be robust; that is, committed to a
point of view about the future shaping of your industry, but capable of
flexing to accommodate the many surprises which will emerge over
time.

Apart from strategic planning, what else can you do if you want to
start taking charge of your future? You could try the following three
prescriptions, which are developed in a little more detail below.

1. Develop a richer understanding of the forces shaping your industry's
   future.
2. Identify, and start to build, sources of competitive advantage which
   are robust enough to create superior customer value in a range of
   possible futures.
3. Build a human organisation which can respond swiftly and effectively to unforeseen changes.

1. Develop a richer understanding of the forces shaping your industry's future.

Many successful companies are still driven by the vision and insight of the original entrepreneur. Problems can arise when that vision is no longer valid, but there is no mechanism for finding and developing a new one; when there is a Messiah complex, and everyone waits for the unfortunate leader to come up with the Next Great Idea so that they can all follow unquestioningly. The dangers are obvious, and the grave-yards are full of the corpses of businesses that crashed and burned when they reached the limits of the founder's original vision. What can you do to avoid this?

Try **Scenario Thinking**: many management teams now invest significant time in identifying industry driving forces, considering various future projections of these and creating multiple scenarios of potential futures which might develop. The object here is not to *predict* likely futures, but to better develop the ability to think about the future, recognise emerging patterns in streams of events and anticipate their implications in relation to proposed strategies. In Royal Dutch Shell, where much of the pioneering work was done on scenarios, the first objective was to enable the company to develop strategies robust enough to cope with a variety of alternative futures. For more on this, see van der Heijden (1996).

It is also important to get a broader set of inputs into the strategy discussion. These can come from other members of the management team, and, more generally, from other members of staff; they may have insights and data which can challenge comfortable assumptions and stimulate the search for more creative solutions.

2. Identify, and start to build, sources of competitive advantage which are robust enough to create superior customer value in a range of possible futures.

The idea here is to build sources of strength which will last beyond the present short-term opportunity and confer long-term benefits. These may come in the form of distinctive capabilities, growth-enabling skills, unique assets (for example patents, access to supply or distribution channels, optimum locations) and networks/alliances.

3. Build a human organisation which can respond swiftly and effectively to unforeseen changes.

Clearly, an adaptable and agile organisation has to be constantly poised for change, which it must execute in a smooth and co-ordinated way. In most cases, this will imply a flattish structure, with decisions devolved as close as possible to the operational front line.

In rapid change, detailed rules and procedures are too rigid and unwieldy; tight co-ordination has to be achieved by competent and self-managed staff members who are guided instead by an understanding of the *principles* which inform the company's strategy and operations. This is yet another argument for having an ongoing and inclusive discussion of the company's future vision and strategy.

A good metaphor and mental image here is one of a shoal of small fish swimming along a tropical reef; a predator appears on the left of the picture, and FLASH! – in an instant the whole shoal is fleeing in the opposite direction. They don't have a discussion and then follow the leader; no, each one sees the problem, each draws the same conclusion, each knows exactly what to do and does it instantly. The shoal survives.

IS THERE ONE BEST WAY TO MAKE STRATEGY?

This book proposes a rational approach to strategy-making, one which provides an analytical framework as a foundation for the manager's energy, creativity, intuition and experience-based insights. We believe that this rational approach is effective in most business situations. Many people argue that in fast-changing industries, managers must think on their feet, respond constantly to major shifts, and re-make their strategies as they go. However true this may be for your industry, any strategy you make will be sounder if it is based on a deep understanding of your company and the forces in your business environment.

The approach we offer can be summarised in four phases:

Direction-setting   In this phase, the company defines the scope of its future business and sets its long-term goals.

Analysis   In this phase, the company looks in detail at the likely future development of its business environment, examines the company's current situation and strengths, and identifies some priority areas for attention.

Strategy-making   In this phase, the company considers the options available, decides on the main thrusts which will drive its long-term strategy, and identifies key interim actions and progress measures.

Implementation   In this phase, the company arranges necessary resources, makes detailed action plans for the next six to twelve months and manages the ongoing progress of the strategy.

On paper this looks like a linear process, with a lot of talking and analysis before any action takes place. In practice, however, the **analysis** and **strategy-making** phases are revisited frequently as environmental conditions change, and the details of the strategy are adjusted accordingly.

ARE THERE ALTERNATIVE APPROACHES TO DEVELOPING STRATEGIES?

Corporate and business strategy has been a hot topic for most of the last half-century, so there have been a number of waves of thought. In the early days – the 1950s and early 1960s – the competitive environment was pretty stable and predictable, and business planners were able to forecast the future quite well by extrapolating past trends forward. Then in the 1960s, markets started to behave more unpredictably as consumer choice widened and international competition intensified. As we moved towards the 1970s, companies started to invest in **strategic planning,** which now involved scanning for trends in environmental change. And that seemed fine for a while. But as we moved through the 1980s, it was noticed that expensively-produced strategic plans often gathered dust on high shelves while the company followed some other course of action which seemed to have emerged from God-knows-where.

Emergent Strategy

Analysis of the planning problem led to the observation that you could not predict the far future with great accuracy; and if you planned on the assumption that you could do so, your plan would gradually decay into irrelevance. The increasingly irrelevant plan would be re-shaped and adjusted by managers who were trying to cope with the unpredicted business realities now emerging in front of them. Thus the strategy which was finally realised consisted of a blend of the planned one and the improvised or "emergent" one (as Professor Henry Mintzberg called it).

One lesson here was that, while you may plan to a long time horizon, you should incorporate frequent reality reviews, and your core strategy should be robust enough to remain valid for a wide range of conditions.

Three Modes of Strategy-Making

Mintzberg went on to observe that not all companies make strategy through a process of **Planning**, although most people think of planning as almost synonymous with strategy. Some companies, for instance, are driven mostly in an **Entrepreneurial** mode, often by a dominant leader who has a compelling vision and is impatient to move quickly and grasp the opportunity. This mode is associated with high levels of energy and excitement, and also with high risk. Finally, some companies make their strategies neither by Planning nor by Entrepreneurial drive, but by **Adapting and Reacting**. Without either a strong vision or a deliberate plan, they seek to continue on their quiet way, ready to cope as best they can with whatever challenges the world throws at them. Usually, they achieve this by holding flexible resources and a fair bit of slack, which usually makes them less efficient.

What is really useful about all this is not the knowledge that any of these extreme modes might appear in companies, but the fact that a robust strategy-making process probably needs a mixture of all three modes. Thus, a Planning-only approach will lack vision, energy and excitement, while a pure Entrepreneurial approach will be dangerously lacking in rigour and balance; a blend of the two is a better option.

But even a great plan in pursuit of a compelling vision is unrealistic if it does not recognise that often the future will not turn out as expected, and therefore the strategy had better contain some mechanism for coping with unforeseen elements. This could take the form of slack resource, or a management team which is unusually well skilled in crisis management, or a workforce which is multi-skilled and can cope with varied demands.

Strategic Intent and Core Competences

Some quite new ideas about strategy-making were advanced around 1990 by Professors Gary Hamel and CK Prahalad in a series of articles in the Harvard Business Review. These were based in large part on their observations of a number of companies, many of them Japanese, which had achieved outstanding global success over recent decades. Hamel and Prahalad noted that in the companies they studied, there was little adherence to the disciplines of strategic planning as practised in much of the Western business world; on the contrary, these companies' development was driven by a couple of powerful focusing devices. The first of these was what the authors called Strategic Intent.

Strategic Intent meant that an organisation such as Honda, Sony or Komatsu would set itself an almost impossibly ambitious goal for a point in the far future. An example was Honda's ambition to "Be the second Henry Ford", at a time when Honda was a tiny company making engines for motor-assisted bicycles in post-war Japan. The goal was so enormous, and so long-range, that it could not be planned for, but it had an important value. First, when it was repeated often enough, with sufficient conviction, people started to believe in it and to be energised by it. Second, it created a strong sense of "misfit" – a focus on what competences and resources Honda lacked and would have to build, if it were ever to emulate Ford. This "stretch" agenda was the underlying basis of Honda's development for 40 years, and was well understood by everyone in the company.

Having high ambition does not of itself ensure success, but great success seldom comes to companies which set modest goals. As Hamel observes: "Firms rarely outperform their aspirations". One outcome of strategic intent is that it can identify the need to build certain core capabilities and competences.

Core Competence is a uniquely superior ability a firm may possess to perform one or more critical value-creating activities. When it is difficult for a company to invent a strategy which is superior to and distinctive from its rivals, its best alternative is to beat them with superior strategy implementation. Building Core Competences which competitors cannot equal is a good way to do this. It involves managing human skills and knowledge bases, building work teams and linking the know-how and activities of various work groups and departments.

A core competence is a unique bundling of a number of individual skills, which collectively creates a source of unusual customer value over the long term, and can be applied across a range of product applications. Hamel and Prahalad (1994) quote, for instance, Sony's outstanding competence in miniaturisation of electronic products, and Canon's in optics and mechatronics. Honda's Core Competence is identified as its outstanding ability to design and make small four-stroke engines. This is a grouping of many constituent skills and technologies – metallurgy, combustion and so on. All of these individual skills and technologies can be hired freely from the market, and Honda's rivals have just as easy access to them as Honda does. Honda creates its Core Competence by the way it blends and manages these constituents to build a unique source of customer value.

Core Competence is a useful concept which many managers have found intuitively plausible. One of the practical difficulties in its application is the problem of identifying which are the competences which will deliver long-term customer value and therefore business success in the far future. Was it luck that made Honda focus on an area which was to prove pivotal, or was it foresight? And if it was foresight, how was it done?

The Resource-Based Approach to Strategy-Making

The widespread interest in the work of Hamel and Prahalad in the early 1990s reflected the fact that the competitive world had become very turbulent, with ever more rapid changes in markets, technologies and competitors. Companies that established a particular positioning in the market found that the market changed quickly and radically, requiring them to move to a new positioning. In a world where the speed of environmental change was outpacing the ability of companies to adapt to it, managers began to look for an alternative model. Instead of trying to anticipate the likely medium-term swings and whims of the environment, and then scramble to prepare a strategic response, the new model would try to identify strategic levers for the company which would hold good over a longer time-span. And with these levers, the company could to some extent *shape* the environment rather than always having to adapt to it. This search gave rise to the resource-based view, on which much has been written by consultants and business school professors; it also owes a lot to the work of Hamel and Prahalad.

The resource-based view takes the position that competition in the future is likely to be heavily based on long-term company capabilities rather than on how the company decides to position itself in the market, and these capabilities will tend to fall under the following headings:

1. **Distinctive Capabilities**: these are related to the Core Competences described above.
2. **Privileged Assets**: these are assets/resources to which the company has unique access. They may include patents, licences, access to scarce inputs, distribution channels, landing rights, excellent retail locations and so on.
3. **Growth-Enabling Skills**: it could be argued that these overlap with Distinctive Capabilities, but they are usually looked at separately.

    An example here would be an organisational talent and set of routines for making mergers and acquisitions work smoothly and profitably every time.

4. **Networks and Alliances**: in an age when many companies are collaborating in the creation of integrated supply chains and partnerships, this is an obvious source of long-term strength.

If the company has managed to amass enough of the right resources in advance, then it should be better positioned to create customer value and outperform its competitors in the future marketplace. The difficulty lies with identifying which resources are likely to be central to future value creation and should therefore be developed/acquired, as companies still have to choose how to deploy limited resources. Since these strategic resources, once identified, take time to develop, management is still left with the problem of speculating about what the far future will look like; and there are no easy answers here.

CHAPTER TWO

Vision, Business Definition and Goals

Creating a strategic vision
Business definition
Setting long-term goals for the organisation
The company's philosophy and values

"To accomplish great things, we must not only act, but also dream; not only plan, but also believe."

Anatole France

CREATING A STRATEGIC VISION

A Strategic Vision is a view of what the organisation's key stakeholders want it to be at a future time. It consists of two basic and separate elements:

1. Future Business Definition

This is a statement which aims to define what business(es) the company wishes and does not wish to engage in. It describes the company's role or **purpose** in the world. A business can only exist if it creates real value for a customer, and Business Definition answers the question: what value will we create, and for what customers? Sometimes companies start by defining their business as "making a profit". But this is not of much use as a definition. Profit is a **result** of the company's creation of value for customers. "Making a profit" tells us nothing about where or how it is to be made. What makes one business different from another, even from those in the same industry, is not that it makes a profit – all companies must do that – but how it will do so, that is, doing what and for whom?

2. Long-Term Goals

These are the few key markers by which the company will ultimately recognise strategic success or failure. They may include such measures as profitability, growth, reputation and industry leadership.

Is a Vision Necessary?

Without a clear and agreed vision, leaders and managers have no guide to keep them oriented to a common purpose; no criteria to decide whether to pursue this opportunity rather than that one. The organisation loses focus and drifts along in no particular direction. A clear strategic vision provides an overview of what the company is all about and where it is headed. It is the starting point for effective strategic leadership. It answers the question: **what** do we want to be and to achieve? Only when the key stakeholders have decided this does it make sense to consider **how** it is to be done. Unfortunately, there is still plenty of evidence of companies trying to address the **how** before getting the **what** clear. Examples we see are: a scattered portfolio of products or businesses which do not seem to hang together or to be going anywhere; new markets entered, then reversed out of; major restructurings implemented, then revised radically by the next set of consultants to come on the scene; a sense of drift in the organisation, even in the midst of frenetic activity.

BUSINESS DEFINITION

The Business Definition is the starting point for any disciplined approach to making strategy. Some people like to refer to this as the organisation's Mission. Often, however, the word "mission" means different things to people, and this can lead to fogginess and confusion. Many corporate mission statements are quite vague about defining the business, while they have a lot to say about the company's espoused values and aspirations; undoubtedly some of these are written more for public consumption than for use as a guideline by company managers.

It is, of course, important to identify the underlying values and beliefs of the company, and we will discuss these below. But at this stage let us be clear:

Business Definition/Mission should define, as explicitly as possible, what business or businesses the company will engage in, and which it will not.

Derek F Abell (1980) produced a model which enables a company to define its business along three dimensions:

1. Which **customer** groups will we serve?
2. Which **needs** of those customers will we aim to satisfy?
3. With what **technologies/competences/services** will we do it?

Figure 2.1 Abell's Framework for Defining the Business

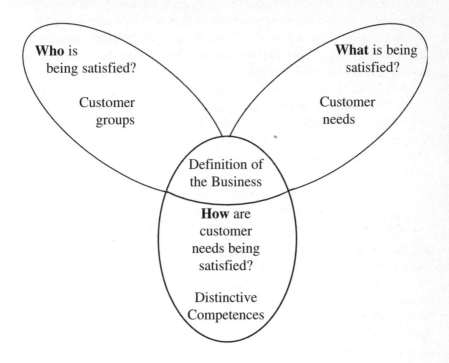

The key decisions here are about choice. You can't do everything for everyone and be the best in class across the board. You have to choose. The hard part is deciding whom you are **not** interested in serving in the future, and which needs you are **not** so interested in addressing. What you are trying to do here is to define the core area where the business will aim to create distinctive and outstanding customer value. This is the area in which you will strive to build (and renew) long-term competitive advantage.

What is particularly useful about Abell's model is that it takes a **customer-focused** rather than a product-based approach. Thus the first question aims to identify which customers, and the second tries to identify the customer needs. Only then do we think about the competences, technologies and products which might be relevant here.

Historically, it was common for companies to define their business in terms of their current product or technology set, without much regard for whether these continued to match customer needs; and many illustrious companies bit the dust as a result. Back in 1960, the marketing guru Theodore Levitt wrote this cautionary account of the decline of the once-great US railroad companies:

> The railroads did not stop growing because the need for passenger and freight transportation declined. That grew. The railroads are in trouble today not because the need was filled by others (cars, trucks, airplanes, even telephones), but because it was not filled by the railroads themselves. They let others take customers away from them because they assumed themselves to be in the railroad business rather than in the transportation business. The reason they defined their industry wrong was because they were railroad oriented rather than transport oriented; they were product oriented instead of customer oriented.

20/20 hindsight is truly a great gift, but if the railroads had been primarily focused on customers and on how best to address their growing needs, they might have taken note of new options and technologies in transportation. They could then have used their reputations and considerable resources to build dominant positions in today's road transport and logistics industries. Instead, most of them declined and went out of business.

For a modern example, consider the current world-wide revolution in retail financial services. As nations deregulate, incumbent companies who remain wedded to their established patterns of service find themselves left behind by nimbler competitors – many of whom are new entrants to the area. The new winners are happy to discard old constraints and follow the customers' needs, with more flexible opening hours, delivery channels and product options.

Illustrative Excerpts from Business Definitions

- Selling clothing for the family, homeware, and a range of fine foods – all representing high standards of quality and value. (Marks & Spencer)

- To invest in good quality basic businesses providing essential goods and services for the consumer and industry. (Hanson)

- Our objective is to achieve profitable growth and long term customer satisfaction by selling a quality range of meat and meat products, offering honest product value from a clean environment and a friendly efficient service. (An Irish Meat Company)

- ...concentrated on developing high-quality products which make unique technological contributions and are so innovative that customers are willing to pay premium prices. Products are limited to the areas of electronic testing and measurement and to technologically related fields. Customer service, both before and after the sale, is given primary emphasis. (Hewlett-Packard in the 1980s)

Identifying Customer Needs

"Customer focus" is more than a slogan. If you really want to know what your customers' needs are, you need first of all to become more intimate with your customers. One way to get started on this is to stop thinking of "the customers" as a homogeneous mass, and to look instead for a set of recognisable sub-groups or segments. It is usually possible to think more precisely about the needs of a member of a segment; it is also easier to target your market research.

Suppose you are planning to set up a short-haul airline, and you want to think about customer needs. You could identify your potential customers as "members of the travelling public", or even "air travellers", but it does not get you very far; the grouping is too broad, and you cannot get down to the fine levels of need where you can discover opportunities to create real value and outflank the incumbent competitors. But suppose you go one stage further, and create separate segments for "business people", "tourists", "family visiting friends and relatives"? Now you can look more closely at the needs of each group separately, noting the importance each group assigns to different aspects of the service – price, punctuality, flight frequency, food and drink, ease of booking, check-in, wheelchairs, friendly service and so on. You can compare where their priority needs differ and, perhaps more importantly, where they converge. This enables you to design a service package which will meet the most keenly-felt needs of a large section of the potential customer base – a powerful planning base for competitive advantage.

SETTING LONG-TERM GOALS FOR THE ORGANISATION

Business Definition describes the arena in which the company hopes to operate in the future; goals refer to the results the company aims to achieve in that arena. To put it another way: **goals** are statements of the long-term benefits the company hopes to realise. They may not all be numerate or precisely quantifiable, but they should be **real and observable**. They are the criteria by which the company will recognise long-term success.

- Goals should be few in number. If you have twenty goals you have no goals;
- They should be stretching, a little ambitious;
- They should be stimulating, energising, exciting;
- They should be ranked in priority order;
- They should be stated in the present tense at a future time;
- They are ends, not means;
- They are not short-term; their time frame is that of the strategic vision, usually four or more years out.

Most firms will have a **profit or profitability** goal: this should be explicit and numerate. The majority of firms will have a **growth** goal (such as rate of growth, share of market/segment, dominance, leadership); again, this should be explicit and quantified. Other goals may include, for example technological excellence, innovation, intellectual leadership, preferred employment for most talented people, creation of local community wealth/stability, best quality of service in the sector and so on. These are less explicitly measurable, and surrogate measures may need to be created; what is important is that achievement or non-achievement of the goal should be clearly observable, as should progress towards the goal.

Some Examples of Long-Term Goals

- To run businesses which are number one or number two in their global markets. (General Electric)

- To achieve 100 per cent total customer satisfaction...every day...in every restaurant...for every customer. (McDonalds)

- 30 per cent of the company's annual sales must come from products fewer than four years old. (3M Corporation)

- To maintain an average earnings per share growth rate of 15 per cent per year. (McCormick & Company)

THE COMPANY'S PHILOSOPHY AND VALUES

Earlier in this section, we noted that a Business Definition is often accompanied by a statement of the organisation's values and beliefs, and that these two elements together form a mission statement.

Why have a Values Statement?

Why indeed? You can develop a perfectly good strategy, and go on to write a perfectly fine strategic plan, on the strength of a clear business definition and a focused set of goals. Many companies do just that, and do not address the values issue. However, an increasing number of companies do. Why? Every organisation has its own set of underlying beliefs and values, whether or not these are ever articulated, much less written down. These are a major part of the culture of the organisation, which helps to shape the attitudes, behaviours and aspirations of the members at all levels. So, whether we notice it or not, the values of the organisation are likely to be driving the decisions about business definition, goal-setting and strategy. The stronger the culture is, the more it is likely to influence management's strategic choices and responses. If we accept that this is so, it may be wise to try to become more conscious of what these values and beliefs really are (rather than what we would like to think they are) and ultimately to try to manage their development. Strong cultural influences are a part of the reason why some companies develop reputations for particular strategic characteristics, such as obsession with quality, passion for technological leadership, focus on customer service, ability to attract the best and brightest talent and so on. Values statements provide a foundation, then, for culture building and for guiding the behaviour of people at all levels in the organisation.

At its best, a values statement can give organisation members a higher sense of purpose in their work, and this can result in better job satisfaction, higher motivation and a greater propensity to contribute to the shaping and fulfilment of the strategy. Clearly, this can only happen when the values described are truly being lived or actively promoted. If this is not seen to be so, and the statement is merely some sort of PR document, the resulting loss of credibility will extend to other aspects of the strategy. It will lower trust in management and impede future organisational change efforts.

Typical Elements of Values Statments

- Commitment to customers;
- Ethical position, commitment to honesty, fairness, integrity;

- Concern for employees, their development and fulfilment, respect for their views, desire for their contribution/participation;
- Focus on quality of product/service;
- Commitment to creativity and innovation;
- Service orientation;
- Obligations to the community and to the environment;
- Duties to customers and suppliers;
- Responsibility to shareholders.

Sample Extracts from Values Statements

- We believe our first responsibility is to the doctors, nurses and patients, to mothers and fathers and all others who use our products and services. (Johnson & Johnson)

- To our employees and those who may join us...we pledge personal respect, fair compensation, and equal treatment. We acknowledge our obligation to provide able and humane leadership throughout the organisation, within a clean and safe working environment. To all who qualify for advancement, we will make every effort to provide opportunity. (Bristol-Myers Squibb)

CHAPTER THREE

Gaining Competitive Advantage

Value and generic strategies
The building blocks of competitive advantage
The value chain

"Competitive advantage is based not on doing what others already do well, but on doing what others cannot do as well."

John Kay, London Business School

The central aim in making strategy is to gain competitive advantage over competitors. Companies which have competitive advantage in an industry enjoy higher margins than the industry average. We used to talk of **sustainable competitive advantage** as the Holy Grail of business strategy, but it becomes increasingly difficult to sustain specific advantages over time. Eventually, rivals will emulate or substitute most of your innovations, cancelling your competitive edge. So it may be that most advantages are transitory, and long-term success depends on being able to innovate continually, so creating successive waves of advantage. This requires leadership and organisation which is capable of strategy innovation, and a business approach which stimulates the drive to create new value.

VALUE AND GENERIC STRATEGIES

Businesses exist to create value for customers. If they do this efficiently, they prosper; if not, they fail. Value can be created by increasing customer benefits, or by lowering customer cost. Michael Porter, writing in 1980, proposed that firms seeking to succeed in an industry should first examine the industry and assess the forces operating in it. From this they should then decide how to position themselves, so as to gain sustainable competitive advantage in either of two basic ways: Low Cost or Differentiation.

Low Cost producers aim to capture a large share of the market, usually with an offer of low prices. Typically they offer adequate quality, but without frills or a wide range of options. They use their high volumes to create cost efficiencies via economies of scale. The extra margins thus created may be passed on to the customer in lower prices – thus cementing and building future sales volumes – or some of it may be taken as extra profit.

Differentiators, on the other hand, aim to identify significant segments in the markets that are prepared to pay a little more (sometimes more than a little) for a product or service which goes further toward meeting their particular needs. This may be seen in a wider range of product choice, higher quality standards, technological superiority, better service support, or simply the reassurance and cachet of a strong brand.

Porter argued (and still does) that companies need to choose between these two basic strategies, as it is very difficult to excel in both at the same time. Firms who try to straddle both strategies can end up "stuck in the middle", not quite as efficient as the dedicated Low Cost players, and not as distinctive as the dedicated Differentiators. Ultimately they may find that they cannot compete and get squeezed out.

Low Cost operators and Differentiators target the whole market, but Porter noted that a third type of player might compete using a niche or *Focus* strategy. Focus players target only a limited but defined segment of the market and attempt to meet the needs of that segment inimitably. Focus can take various forms or themes:

- Low Cost Focus, for those for whom economy is extremely important, for example discount grocery stores, car makes from low-wage countries;
- Differentiation Focus, for people who will pay seriously above the odds for the exclusive and distinctive, for example Porsche cars, Rolex watches;
- Geographic focus, where there are specialised regional tastes or requirements, or where transport costs favour local manufacture, for example concrete blocks.

Figure 3.1 Porter's Generic Strategies Model

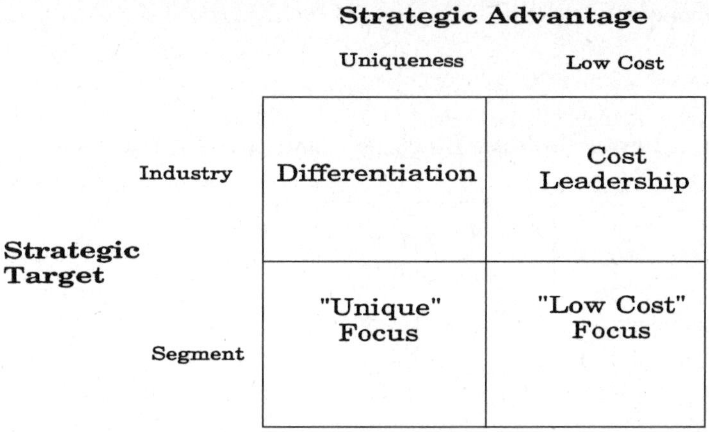

Strategic Advantage

	Uniqueness	Low Cost
Industry	Differentiation	Cost Leadership
Segment	"Unique" Focus	"Low Cost" Focus

Strategic Target

Reprinted with the permission of the Free Press, a division of Simon of Schuster, Inc. from *Competitive Strategy: techniques for analyzing industries and competitors* by Michael E Porter. Copyright © 1980, 1998 by the Free Press.

Albeit an extremely simple idea, business people have found Porter's model very useful in clarifying their thinking about strategic choice. Many managers, however, have got to the point of deciding to pursue a Low Cost or a Differentiation strategy and have then found themselves wondering "but where do I start?"

THE BUILDING BLOCKS OF COMPETITIVE ADVANTAGE

Hill and Jones (1995) added an extremely helpful development of the model with their *Building Blocks of Competitive Advantage*. This framework gives four basic ways in which companies can gain advantage:

1. Superior Efficiency;
2. Superior Quality;
3. Superior Customer Responsiveness;
4. Superior Innovation.

In everyday speech, we often use the word "superior" to mean something is very good indeed, whereas it really means "better than". In the competitive world, being very good does not mean a whole lot; being better than your opposition is what counts. So when we claim "Superior

Quality", we are talking about quality which is better than that of our competitors and is seen by our customers as better.

As shown below, the four Building Blocks feed into Low Cost and Differentiation:

Figure 3.2 Four Building Blocks of Competitive Advantage

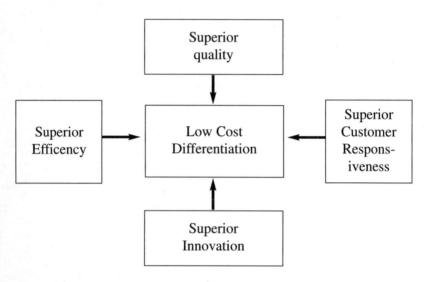

Hill, Charles W & Gareth Jones, *Strategic Management Theory,* Third Edition, Copyright © 1995 by Houghton Mifflin Company. Used by permission.

The four factors are not entirely independent of each other: an improvement in quality, for example, may reduce costs (efficiency) and also add to customer responsiveness. It is interesting to note, however, that each one of the four has, in turn, been identified as the prime source of competitive edge over the last few decades. Thus in the 1970s, companies pursued Cost Efficiency through industrial engineering and scale economies; in the 1980s and early 1990s "Quality" was the mantra, and we adopted TQM and ISO; this was closely followed by Customer Service and Responsiveness; and now, in the new century, Innovation is seen to be the key driver of advantage.

This does not mean that some of the earlier factors are not important; quite the opposite, in fact. Today, if you are not efficient and your quality is not excellent, you will not even be in the game; these are merely the price of admission. Having got in, you must then decide how you will get an edge on the others.

Innovation is probably the ultimate source of competitive advantage, whether the innovation be in products, marketing approach, organisation, management systems, technologies or strategies. All around us we see companies whose outstanding success is linked to innovation: Intel, Hewlett-Packard, Sony in technology; Dell with an innovative business system and route to market; Southwest Airlines and Ryanair with a new price/performance equation.

So where do the Building Blocks of Competitive Advantage get us to? Say we have decided that our company would like to position itself strategically as a Differentiated supplier in the market and we are wondering where to start. One way might be to ask: what mix of factors do we need to excel at, and to what degree? If we take the Building Blocks as our guide, we might decide that we need to be at the average industry standard on some, better than most competitors on others and uniquely excellent on another. For instance, this could mean being about average on Efficiency, somewhat above on Quality, better than most on Innovation and outstandingly unique on Customer Responsiveness.

Having decided to aim for this kind of positioning, we would then need to figure out how to do it, that is what capabilities and resources do we need to build to get us to the desired level on each factor? We could approach this in a fairly unstructured or brainstorming sort of way. Thus, if we aim to be utterly outstanding on Customer Responsiveness, we might spontaneously identify the following necessities:

Resources	Flexible manufacturing system; Customer-focused leadership; Rapid-response supply chain; Staff with appropriate innate disposition; Customer feedback process.
Capabilities	To promote a customer-focused culture; To process customer information swiftly; To respond rapidly in manufacturing and logistics; To involve customers in product development; To develop staff in customer responsiveness.

Alternatively, we could use a structured or graphic model to prompt our thinking and integrate the constituent pieces of our developing strategy.

Many people have found a value chain model useful for this purpose, and probably the best-known model is that developed by Michael Porter and described in his book *Competitive Advantage* (1985).

THE VALUE CHAIN

Value chain analysis aims to trace the value created in different stages of a process. If we look at an industry in this way, we see that the creation of value for the end-customer is a process shared among many firms at various stages on the way from raw materials to retail sale. If we place our own firm within this value system, it may help us to gain a new perspective on our role in creating value for the end-customer. It might stimulate thinking about how we might work differently with partners – suppliers, purchasers, even perhaps with competitors – to create a better value proposition for end customers, that is one which offers them lower total costs or better service/functionality. There are many examples of this in practice: just-in-time deliveries; joint marketing programmes; industry consortia such as Airbus Industrie.

Figure 3.3 The Industry Value System

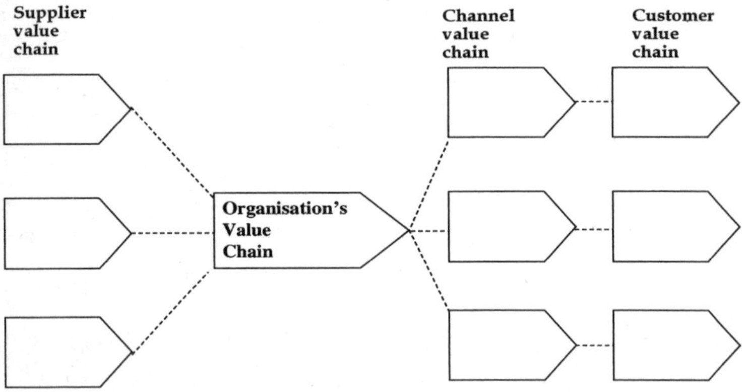

Reprinted with permission from Gerry Johnson & Kevan Scholes. *Exploring Corporate Strategy,* Second Edition, London: Prentice-Hall, 1988, p.87. Adapted from M E Porter, *Competitive Advantage.* Used with permission of the Free Press, a Division of Simon & Schuster, Inc., from *Competitive Advantage: creating and sustaining superior performance* by Michael E Porter. Copyright © 1985, 1988 by Michael E Porter.

At the level of the firm itself, we can analyse the value-creating activities using Porter's Generic Value Chain framework. Porter (1985) maintains that firms derive competitive advantage from their ability to perform value-creating activities particularly well and to gain leverage by managing linkages between these activities. The exhibit below is a representation of the value chain for a typical firm which might be in manufacturing. For firms in other kinds of businesses, the titles of the various activities should be changed as appropriate.

Primary Activities

Primary activities are those that are directly related to the creation or delivery of a product or service. They are grouped under five headings:

1. Inbound Logistics (receiving, checking, storing inputs to the business);
2. Operations (transforming the inputs into the final product or service);
3. Outbound Logistics (warehousing, distribution and so on);
4. Marketing and Sales (self-explanatory);
5. Service (activities which enhance or maintain the value of the product while it is in the hands of the customer).

Support Activities

Support Activities help to enhance the effectiveness of Primary Activities. In this model there are four categories:

1. Procurement (processes for acquiring inputs to various parts of the business);
2. Technology Development (activities which improve either the product/service or the process);
3. Human Resource Management (recruitment, staff development, rewards);
4. Firm Infrastructure (leadership, structure, information and control systems, planning and finance, management style and routines).

Figure 3.4 The Generic Value Chain

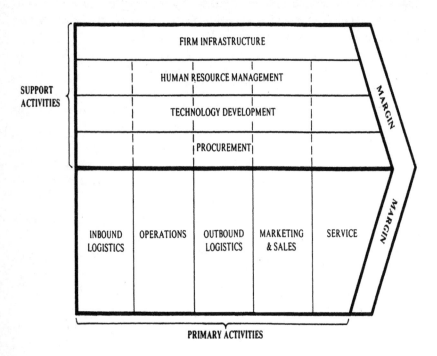

Reprinted with permission of the Free Press, a division of Simon & Schuster, Inc., from *Competitive Advantage: creating and sustaining superior performance* by Michael E Porter. Copyright© 1985, 1988 by Michael E Porter.

The idea here is not to fill up all the boxes with lists of the activities carried out in each area; quite the contrary. What we need to do is to start with some clarity about the value we want to create for the customer, then "reverse engineer" this in terms of which *few key activities*, or combination of activities, will do most to create that value. Remember Pareto's Principle: many companies spend probably 80 per cent of their effort and funds on activities which do little to enhance real customer value. The Value Chain is a lens which may enable you to look with fresh eyes at how effectively you are converting resources into value.

By way of illustration, below is a Value Chain rendering of the activities of Kwik-Save, a UK discount store chain which is committed to a highly-focused low-cost strategy.

In this example, the company has used the Value Chain to isolate those few key activities with which it will deliver low cost. It has also made clear choices about omitting activities (such as Service) which do not contribute directly toward that end.

Figure 3.5 Kwik-Save

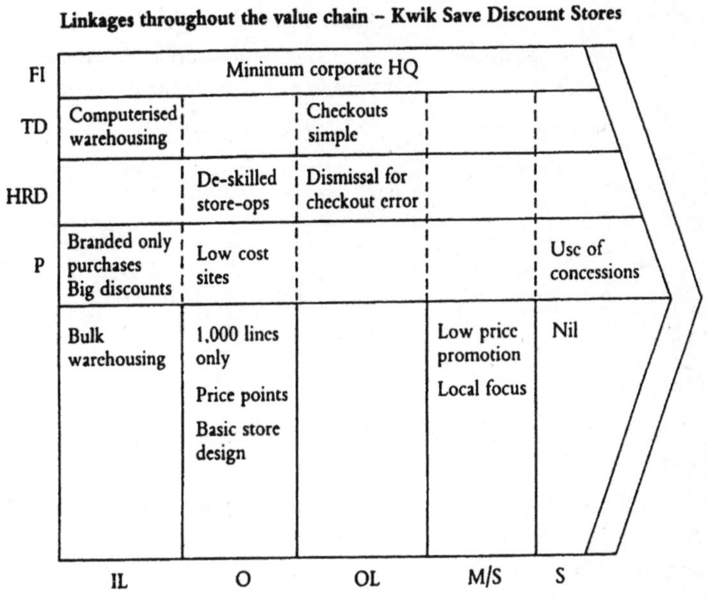

Linkages throughout the value chain – Kwik Save Discount Stores

	IL	O	OL	M/S	S
FI	Minimum corporate HQ				
TD	Computerised warehousing		Checkouts simple		
HRD		De-skilled store-ops	Dismissal for checkout error		
P	Branded only purchases Big discounts	Low cost sites			Use of concessions
	Bulk warehousing	1,000 lines only Price points Basic store design		Low price promotion Local focus	Nil

Source: *Kwik-Save Discount.* A case study by Derek Channon, Manchester Business School. Reproduced with permission from G Johnson and K Scholes, *Exploring Corporate Strategy*, Second Edition, p.92, Prentice-Hall.

CHAPTER FOUR

Analysing the External Environment

The macro-environment
The industry environment
- industry analysis
- strategic groups
- competitor analysis
Summarising the Environmental Review
Surprises, and the need for divergent thinking
Working with scenarios

"War is ninety per cent information."

Napoleon Bonaparte

"You can observe a lot just by watching."

Yogi Berra

In looking at the external environment of the organisation, we need to identify and examine all the entities in the outside world which might help or hinder us in achieving our long-term goals. What we are trying to do here is to spot sources of opportunity or threat. Because we are taking the long view, we need to consider these external entities not just as they are now, but as they might develop and change over the time-span of our strategy. Some of these changes could be caused directly by actions we ourselves might take over the coming period.

If the environment is "everything outside the organisation", it is a pretty big field, and we can evaluate it more systematically if we use some frameworks to guide our questioning. It is useful to think of the company's environment at two levels. The first is that of the **industry** in which we are operating, and here we look at those with whom we interact directly to make a profit or loss. Outside of that, the industry sits within a larger set of entities which we will call the **macro-environment**. The diagram below illustrates this.

Figure 4.1 The External Environment

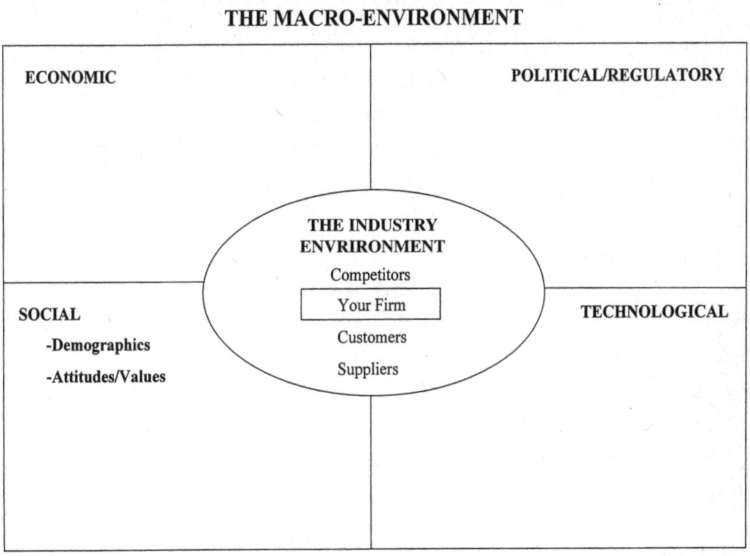

THE MACRO-ENVIRONMENT

ECONOMIC	POLITICAL/REGULATORY

THE INDUSTRY
ENVRIRONMENT

Competitors

Your Firm

Customers

Suppliers

SOCIAL	TECHNOLOGICAL
-Demographics	
-Attitudes/Values	

THE MACRO-ENVIRONMENT

The macro-environment is usually split into four sections for analysis, as shown above: Economic, Political, Social and Technological. Under each of these headings we can then start to identify sub-elements and ask which elements might change during the period of our strategy. We should assess whether such changes would have a significant impact, positive or negative, on our plans.

SECTION	TYPICAL SUB-ELEMENTS
Economic	Growth rates
	Interest rates
	Inflation
Political	Stability
	Taxation policy
	Regulation/Deregulation
Social	
Demographics	Age profiles
	Household formation
	Family size

Attitudes	Work/family balance
	Health
	"Green" issues

Technological	Industry-specific technologies
	New materials
	Telecommunications and information technologies

In general we can say that if the macro-environmental elements are mostly positive to the industry, then the industry as a whole will tend to prosper, and vice versa. However, where adverse macro-environmental conditions create difficulty for the industry as a whole, this may create an opportunity for some players who are better positioned to take advantage of the new conditions. For an example of this, consider the oil crises of the 1970s. The scarcity and high cost of petroleum products hit the motor industry quite hard, especially in the US where cars were big and heavy on fuel. The crisis came at just the right time for the Japanese manufacturers. The small-car niche in the US market suddenly grew massively, just as the Japanese were ready to launch their major export drive. As a result the Japanese producers gained a huge share of the US market which Detroit has never managed to retrieve.

Among the petroleum producers, Royal Dutch Shell improved its position enormously during this period. In Chapter 1 we noted that the company was an early exponent of Scenario Planning. Shell's scenario work enabled managers to interpret the early signs long before the crisis developed fully; they were able to anticipate unfolding events before the other major oil companies and be the first to put forward a coping strategy. The same scenario work enabled Shell to be ready for the world oil glut which developed in the mid-1980s and slashed crude oil prices by two-thirds. By the end of the 1980s Shell had moved from seventh to second place among the world oil companies (see the note on Scenarios at the end of this chapter).

THE INDUSTRY ENVIRONMENT

For most companies it is the forces within the industry which have the greatest impact on the company's fortunes and survival. And these forces are also more susceptible to defence and counter-attack by an alert management team. Therefore it pays to identify and evaluate them.

What are these forces? Essentially they are competitors and players upstream and downstream of the firm in the industry value system. Porter (1980) developed his Five Forces model to represent the play of forces at work in an industry.

Figure 4.2 Porter's Five Forces Model for Industry Analysis

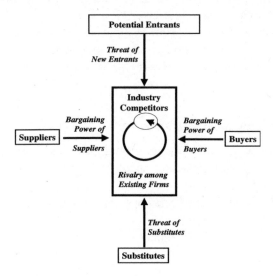

Reprinted with the permission of the Free Press, a Division of Simon & Schuster, Inc., from *Competitive Strategy: Techniques for analyzing industries and competitors* by Michael E Porter. Copyright © 1980, 1988 by the Free Press.

The model shows five forces bearing on a company:

1. Rivalry among established firms in the industry;
2. Threat of new entrants to the industry;
3. Bargaining power of buyers (customers);
4. Bargaining power of suppliers;
5. Threat of substitutes.

In this model, the stronger any of these forces becomes, the more competitive pressure it applies to the company, and the more profit margins are squeezed. If a force looks likely to grow stronger in the future, that constitutes a threat; if it looks likely to weaken for one reason or another, that constitutes an opportunity. One of the objectives in industry analysis is (a) to identify these sources of threat and opportunity, and (b) to find ways to weaken those forces which are seen to be most troublesome.

    It is unusual to find an industry in which all five forces are strong, or one in which all five are weak. What we most commonly find is that in a particular industry there are one or two of the forces which cause most of the problem. In your own business, you could probably name the two dominant forces if you thought about it right now. This is the first step to doing something about it. If you have identified the two most important forces, you can now concentrate on those two and forget about the other three.

The second step is to think about what is driving those two forces. Below we look at some of the factors which drive each of the five forces. It is often possible to counter or weaken a force by focusing on one or more of its driving factors.

Rivalry Among Established Companies

* Industry growth rate: if market growth has slowed or is static, any firm seeking growth must take share from another, thus intensifying rivalry.
* Product differentiation: if no scope can be found for differentiation between the offerings of the various competitors, commodity conditions prevail and price competition results, lowering everyone's margins.
* Switching costs: firms which can "lock in" customers by making it inconvenient or expensive for them to transfer their business elsewhere have effectively limited their competition.
* Large capacity increments: if the nature of the industry means companies have to increase capacity in large "lumps": for instance when a small airline buys a new Boeing 737, the additional capacity may temporarily exceed the natural sales growth. The need for capacity utilisation may drive the company to sell the extra capacity very cheaply and start a price war.
* Capital intensity: linked to the last point; industries which are characterised by high investment in fixed assets tend to be very driven by capacity utilisation needs. When industry volumes turn down, price wars often follow.
* Exit barriers: if there is over-capacity in an industry, it is usually eased by the exit of less profitable companies. Exit barriers prevent this easing and price-cutting may result. Exit barriers arise when companies have expensive and specialised assets for which no real resale market exists; when contractual obligations require continued operation; when labour redundancy costs would be prohibitive; when the owners have strong emotional commitment to carrying on.

The Threat of New Entrants

- Brand or reputation: if incumbents have a strong brand or image with customers, intending entrants may conclude that this is not economically beatable.
- Product differentiation: this connects to the above point.
- Absolute cost advantages: these can arise from various causes such as unique access to raw materials or experience-based efficiencies.
- Patents: possession of patents can make key processes unavailable or prohibitively costly to entrants.
- Technological or competence barriers: the time and costs involved in acquiring necessary skills and technology deters entry.
- Economies of scale: if the industry is characterised by significant scale economies, this will place small entrants at a disadvantage for some time.

In many industries in the past, the threat of entry was identified with small entrepreneurial start-ups, usually driven by people who had experience of the industry. While these could be challenging to incumbents, their growth could be monitored and the incumbents could move against them if they started to look like a real threat. Now, increasingly, we see very large companies broadening their service offerings with surprise moves into new industry sectors, sometimes by acquisition. When one of these arrives suddenly in your industry, the whole landscape can change.

Most of the dedicated firms in the aircraft maintenance business grew out of the airline business, often as subsidiaries of airline companies. On the other hand FLS, one of the major European players in this business, is a large engineering company which moved into aircraft maintenance as a related diversification.

In the airline crisis of the early 1990s, maintenance firms were shocked by the entry into the market of British Airways' and Lufthansa's maintenance divisions. These organisations had previously been exclusively dedicated to their parent airlines; but in order to keep up resource utilisation and to support the parents' profits, they entered the third party market and made this an extremely difficult competitive environment. Many financial service and retail sectors have been upended by Internet firms and firms with innovative selling and distribution approaches. The moral of all this is that New Entrants are not what they used to be, and you need to be wide awake if you are to anticipate the coming competitive threats; they are not all obvious.

The Power of Buyers

- Buyers few and large: when a few buyers command much of the output of the industry, their power is huge – especially so if the industry is fragmented.
- Product differentiation: if a company's product/service is in some way unique, it reduces the buyer's power; the buyer has no alternatives available.
- Switching costs: as before. Lock-ins reduce buyer options and thus buyer power.
- Vertical integration: if the buyers can readily arrange to supply their own needs, they can threaten this to force down prices or resist price increases.
- Buyer information: if the buyer knows the cost structure of the supplying company, sharper price bargaining is likely.
- Buyer profitability: if the buyer's own profit margins are tight, the buyer will fight hard on price.

The Power of Suppliers

- Alternative suppliers: if the supplier's product is an important input and there are few/no alternative sources, supplier power increases.
- Vertical integration: if the supplier is big and can integrate forward, this can force price increases or more demanding supply conditions.
- Product differentiation: as with buyers, but in reverse direction.
- Small customer: when the company is not important to the supplier, it is difficult to negotiate prices, quality or better contract terms.

The Threat of Substitutes

Substitute products are the products of another industry or technology which serve the same customer needs as our company. For example:

- Margarine as a substitute for butter;
- Videos as a substitute for books;
- Mineral water as a substitute for coffee;
- Video conferencing as a substitute for business travel;
- Insulation as a substitute for heating oil.

If close substitutes exist for the company's products, this places some constraints on the freedom to increase prices; witness how many substitutes for oil appeared after the trebling of oil prices in 1979, leading to a price collapse a few years later. If the product has negative features other than price, these can also create conditions for substitution, as with the health issue in relation to butter and other foodstuffs.

Substitution, not direct competition, is often the basis for successful new businesses. Ryanair, a highly successful European low-cost airline, modelled much of its strategy on Southwest Airlines in the US. Both have enjoyed phenomenal passenger growth over the years, but most of this growth has been from entirely new air travellers – people who formerly took surface transport (cars and boats, mostly) or simply did not travel because of the cost and inconvenience. Their growth hurt other airlines a little, but it hit other businesses a lot harder by diverting customer spend to air travel. This poses a question for your own industry: should you be worrying more about your industry competitors, or about someone in some other industry who may some day meet your customers' needs better than you can?

Strategic Groups

If you carry out an industry analysis for your business it should sharpen your understanding of the forces shaping the industry and of how you ought to be trying to position your business in it for maximum advantage. In doing this it is important to be clear about how you define the limits of "the industry". How you define the industry you are in determines who you will focus on as your current and potential competitors; and you need to be really clear about that. For instance Sheraton Hotels, a worldwide company, and the French group Formule 1 are both in the hotel industry, but are they really competitors? And what about BMW and Hyundai? And Coke and 7up? In each case the two companies we look at are not close competitors because they are competing on different bases or with different market focus.

Strategic group analysis tries to sort out the players in an industry according to how they rate on key strategic dimensions, so as to identify groupings of companies whose strategies and positionings are relatively close. For members of such a group the most-felt competition is likely to come from other members of that group or adjacent groups; these are the competitors whose intentions and capabilities should be watched most closely. Examples of strategic dimensions along which industry players may be ranked are:

- Price/quality/image;
- Distribution channels;
- Breadth of product/service range;
- Types of buyers aimed at;
- Degree of vertical integration;
- Intensity of marketing and branding;
- Technological uniqueness;

- Geographical coverage;
- Diversity of parent company.

As an example, we might construct a strategic group map for the watch business using **Price/Image** and **Distribution Channels** as our two dimensions. The various sets of players would then separate as shown below.

Figure 4.3 Strategic Groups

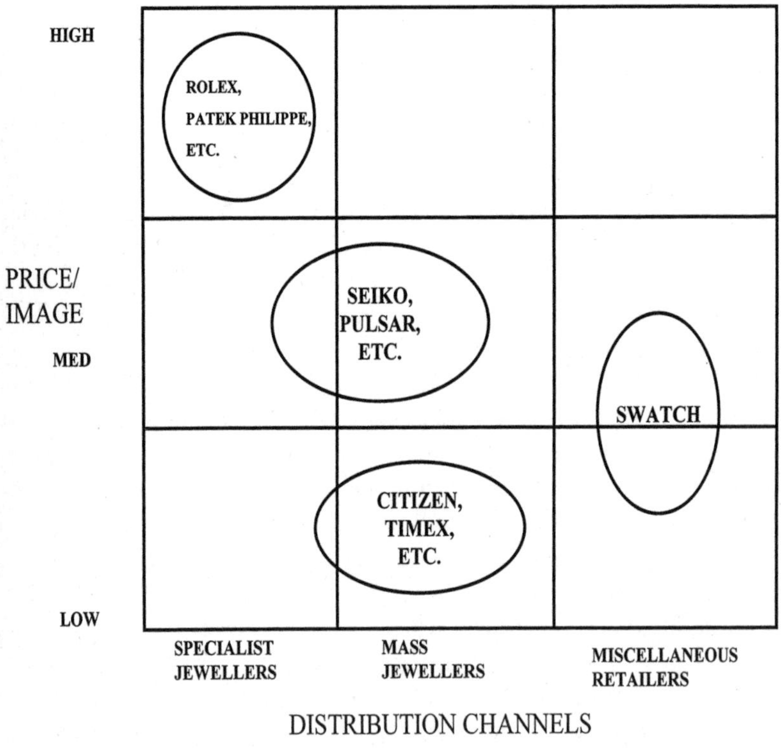

```
HIGH
          ┌─────────────────┐
          │  ROLEX,         │
          │  PATEK PHILIPPE, │
          │  ETC.           │
          └─────────────────┘

PRICE/
IMAGE                    SEIKO,
                         PULSAR,
MED                      ETC.                    SWATCH

                         CITIZEN,
                         TIMEX,
                         ETC.

LOW
        SPECIALIST       MASS
        JEWELLERS        JEWELLERS      MISCELLANEOUS
                                        RETAILERS
```

DISTRIBUTION CHANNELS

In this example we can see how Swatch created a new position for itself by distributing through many kinds of retail outlets (boutiques, sporting goods stores, and so on), rather than limiting itself to jewellery shops. By combining low cost and technical innovation with high style elements, it positioned itself to threaten parts of the middle- and low-priced traditional markets.

Limitations of the Industry Analysis Model

Critics argue that the Five Forces Model is useful only if the industry is in a fairly steady state; that if the rate of innovation in an industry is revolutionary rather than evolutionary the model is of limited use. Porter has acknowledged this objection, and points out that industries go through long periods of gradual change, followed by bursts of rapid change, followed in turn by more gradual change; this is referred to as *punctuated equilibrium*. There are, of course, some high-tech industries where rapid change is so constant that there is no equilibrium – what has been called the arena of *hypercompetition* – and here the model may truly be of limited value.

Competitor Analysis

A key part of any review of the environment is an explicit examination of the position of our main competitors. The object of this is to form a view on (a) what strategies each competitor is most likely to pursue and (b) how each competitor is likely to respond to our moves. The identity of the two or three main competitors may be very obvious and need no further speculation; or it may be that Strategic Group Analysis has given a sharper insight. A further quick test is to ask the question: if we make a significant market move (try to increase sales, drop prices, introduce a new line) who do we think will react?

For each competitor, we need to ask:

How do they see the industry? What growth do they envisage, what major developments, what do they see as central to success, what product and market areas do they value, who do they see as industry leaders, how do they see their own role in the industry? What is the action by us which would provoke them to all-out retaliation?

What are their ambitions? What goals do they aspire to, what has been their growth trajectory in turnover and profits, what can we deduce from their pattern of investments, management recruitment, market research, annual reports, chairman's statements, press releases, rumours in the trade among sales representatives and suppliers?

What is their current strategy? Is there a discernible pattern to their current actions and resource dispositions which makes their intentions clear in regard to market positions, product development, building of new competences or technology? Do they have a strong competitive culture, and how far does it pervade the whole organisation?

What are their strengths and weaknesses? What are their notable strong points? Weak points? How do they compare to us in resources, capabilities, product range, network, organisation and management? Are they better or worse? By how much? What are they doing about it? How are they rated on the things customers really value?

As noted above, the point of all this is to gain a sharper insight into what competition we really face and how each competitor is likely to respond to any strategy which we might bring forth.

SUMMARISING THE ENVIRONMENTAL REVIEW

If you have worked your way through all of these processes, you will have gathered a mass of information and made numerous notes and observations; now what do you do with all this? The ideal aim would be to distil from the mass the few things that really mattered, on which you could now focus management attention and action. There are two ways to do this: identifying Opportunities and Threats, and Key Success Factors.

Opportunities and Threats

As you examined the Macro-Environment (political/regulatory, economic, social, technological), the Industry Analysis (Five Forces model) and Competitor Analysis, you will have noticed a number of situations which you could use to move you toward the goals you have set yourself; or you may have spotted some possible new business areas; or some forces in the environment which you could develop to your strategic advantage. Make a list of all these as Opportunities.

You will also have seen a number of elements which represent potential problems, current or future blockages to the achievement of your goals. Make a list of these as Threats. Keep these two lists; we will return to them later.

Key Success Factors

Each industry, indeed each sub-sector of each industry, has its own set of Key Success Factors – the few central things that determine which will be the most successful firms in that sector. In the fashion clothing industry, for example the key success factors include excellent design capability, close connections to the market and excellent marketing. In the budget hotel sector they will probably include an assurance of consistency (through brand marketing) and locations which are convenient for the targeted user groups.

There are usually only a few real Key Success Factors – typically two to four, with five as a maximum. Possession of these is what distinguishes industry winners from the others. Winning companies usually need to possess **all** of the Key Success Factors and to excel in at least one.

Key Success Factors are usually found in *resources* (staff, location, information systems and so on), *competences* (ability to do certain things uniquely well) or *linkages* (with suppliers, distribution channels, allies).

The real challenge in identifying Key Success Factors is to resist the temptation to include too many. The whole point here is to focus management attention on the few that really matter and then to act on building them stronger. If you include ten factors, you will lose focus and nothing will be achieved. So be tough and rigorous, and agree on three or four. We will return to them later.

SURPRISES, AND THE NEED FOR DIVERGENT THINKING

So far in this book, we have presented a structured approach, with a fair amount of emphasis on analysis. This is all very appropriate and necessary, but structure and analysis will not always be enough on their own. Nor will "me-too" strategies. Increasingly, in a tight, competitive arena, surprises become the norm with new, unexpected competitors and new linkages emerging. The challenge becomes one of anticipating the surprises and being the first in.

What Kinds of Surprises?

* New technology re-shapes the industry value chain, cutting out intermediate stages – a problem confronting retail banks, insurance agents and travel agents.
* Unexpected new entrants, such as Marks and Spencer in financial services and Tesco in petrol retailing.
* Customer needs start to be better served by a new service/product or industry. For instance pre-recorded CDs are under threat from web-based content sources such as Napster/MP3. What is the future for the music store?
* Customer needs disappearing in the face of higher-order innovation. As a simple example, the universal availability of mobile phones has a big impact on companies who operate public phone booths. As utilisation drops, how can they generate new revenue from the sites?

How can you Think More Creatively about all this?

* Let yourself dream a little, speculate on far-fetched possibilities. Read more about emerging technologies and industry trends.
* Try role-play games – get yourself into the heads of your main competitors and think of your company as the enemy: how would you attack your own company?
* Place yourself inside the head of someone who supplies your main customers with the answers to other needs: could their systems replace or obsolete your product or service?
* Find and read stories of major changes in other industries and ask yourself: could any of this happen in my industry? How might it happen? Could I initiate it and gain advantage?
* Try creating some scenarios of different possible futures and devise ways to adapt and thrive in a range of challenging situations (see next section Working with Scenarios).

WORKING WITH SCENARIOS

Scenarios are plausible descriptions of a range of possible futures the organisation might have to deal with. They are built up by selecting the few factors which will be the main drivers of change in the company's environment, projecting alternative ways in which each might develop, then taking different groupings of these to create a set of future pictures. Managers then speculate on what intermediate events and conditions would be needed in order to arrive at a particular future.

Scenario planning is a useful tool when an organisation needs to take a particularly long-term view in its strategy; this may be because of long resource-development cycles in the industry, as in the Shell example referred to earlier. Scenarios usually refer to time horizons of over five years and often in the ten to twenty-year range.

Companies use scenarios to test the robustness of their strategies under a variety of possible conditions in the far future. This is of particular interest where the company is obliged to make binding commitments which have a long pay-back time. To quote Brian Marsh of Shell "The real misunderstanding about scenarios is that they are not a tool for helping our managers predict what will happen, but a means by which we can explore (and learn) about what we should do if it happens!"

The process of working on scenarios also helps managers to think in a more innovative way about the possibilities of future environmental change; they are therefore more likely to challenge current assumptions and "think outside the box".

How is it Done?

The first step is to identify a few key drivers of the future environment which are of *high impact* on the company's strategy and whose future direction is *highly uncertain*. If we identify a large number of factors, the number of possible combinations becomes huge and unmanageable, so it is important to focus on the few really crucial ones.

The second step is to identify possible future states for each factor. Again for the sake of manageability, it is usually better to limit these to two more-or-less opposite states. For example, we might look at *Economic Growth Rate* as *High* or *Sluggish*, or at *Consumer Attitudes to New Technology* as *Enthusiastic* or *Suspicious*.

The third step is to create scenario descriptions based on different combinations of the various factor-states we have set up. Even a small number of factors will produce a large number of potential scenarios; it is normal to pick from among these a few (usually three or four) interesting and diverse ones to build up into a full description.

Figure 4.4 Impact / Uncertainty

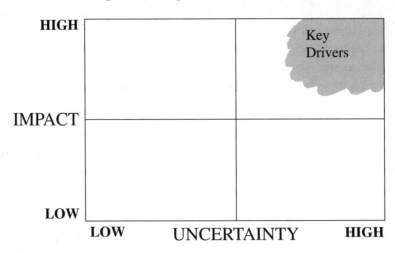

Where the number of potential driving forces is large, companies sometimes use a different approach based on a simple pair of *Optimistic* and *Pessimistic* scenarios, which when fleshed out may develop into more complex "themed stories". Others identify two to four themes at the start, as Shell did when developing strategies for the years 1995-2020, and then build a detailed and internally consistent picture from each.

CHAPTER FIVE

Assessing the Company's Situation

The search approach
McKinsey 7 S model
Portfolio and diversification models

"Whoever desires constant success must change his conduct with the times."

Niccolo Machiavelli

"The downfall of a magician is belief in his own magic"

Anonymous

When we examine the company's situation we look at it in the context of the long-term goals and of the environmental review – including the opportunities and threats we have identified. One of our aims here is to identify the company's areas of strengths and weaknesses, and it is important to note that these are *relative*, that is, a strength is some aspect in which we are *better than* most of our competitors. If we are very good at something but our competitors are also very good, it is not a strength. Likewise, a weakness is an area where we are less good than our main competitors.

THE SEARCH APPROACH

How do we go about looking for areas of relative strength and weakness? To begin with, we should follow the questions in the Workbook section which are arranged under these four headings:

- **Performance Record** – in sales growth, profitability, quality, innovation, efficiency and other indices;
- **Resources** – physical, human, financial, market, product range, relationships/alliances;
- **Capabilities** – unique levels of ability to perform certain value-creating activities;
- **Management and Organisation** – vision, goals, strategy, communications, leadership, management skills, motivation, structure, systems, organisational culture.

Various models and frameworks can help us to tackle this task, and some of the more useful are Porter's Value Chain (described in Chapter 3), the McKinsey 7 S Model, Portfolio Matrices and Diversification Matrices.

MC KINSEY 7 S MODEL

The 7 S Model was originally conceived as a tool for managing strategic change, but it can be helpful as a checklist at this stage. The model looks at an organisation as consisting of seven aspects or facets, each of which must be aligned with the others. These facets are: Strategy, Structure, Systems, Style, Staff, Skills and Shared Values. You will notice that they cover most of the areas mentioned under the four headings above. They are less detailed, but some people find the model attractive for this purpose because it is easy to remember the seven facets all beginning with the letter S.

Figure 5.1   7 S Model

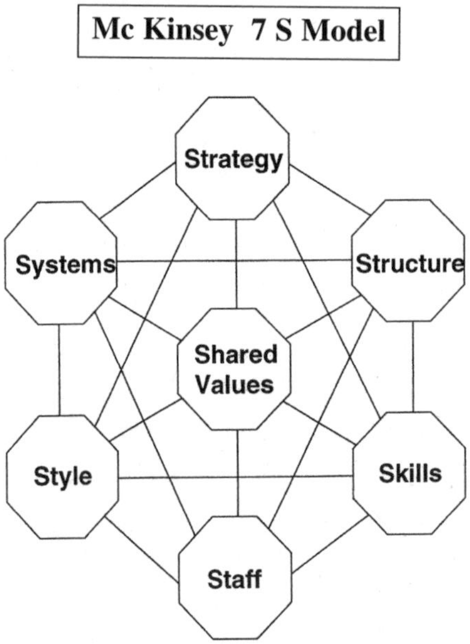

Mc Kinsey 7 S Model

Strategy

Systems

Structure

Shared
Values

Style

Skills

Staff

PORTFOLIO AND DIVERSIFICATION MATRICES

Some of the very earliest models developed to help managers think about corporate strategy were focused on how to get the right mix of businesses or products in the spread of the company's operations. We will look at two of these: the Product/Mission Matrix and the Growth/Share Matrix.

The Product/Mission Matrix

This simple model was created by Igor Ansoff to give companies greater clarity about the degree to which their businesses were diversified (or not) and the implications of the situation. The model looks at the ways companies can grow and deals with four: growth in existing or new markets and growth in existing or new products. These are arranged on two axes to give a four-box matrix as shown:

Figure 5.2 Ansoff's Matrix

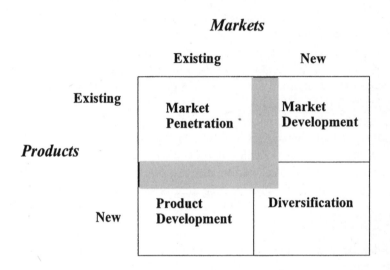

Markets

Source: Igor Ansoff, *Corporate Strategy*. Copyright© 1965 McGraw Hill, Reproduced by permission of John Wiley & Son Inc.

Each of the four boxes is labelled with the strategy choice indicated. The top left-hand box is for Existing Products in Existing Markets and the growth strategy is **Market Penetration**. Here the company is focusing on the core business, and is trying to grow by increasing the number of users.

The top right-hand box is for Existing Products in New Markets and the growth strategy is **Market Development**. Here the company is staying with known technologies and competences, but seeking to take these into unfamiliar market areas; this is therefore a bit more risky than staying in the core business.

The bottom left-hand box is for New Products in Existing Markets and the growth strategy is **Product Development**. The company is staying with the market and customers it knows well, but is aiming to deal in products or technologies with which it is less familiar; this is also a bit more risky than "sticking to the knitting" in the core business.

The bottom right-hand box is for New Products in New Markets and the growth strategy is **Diversification**. Both customers and products/technologies are unfamiliar and this is a doubly risky area of endeavour.

What is the best strategy? On the one hand, some authorities advise companies to "stick to the knitting" and not venture outside; on the other hand, we see companies which seem to prosper in diversification. The available evidence so far suggests that companies who stick in their core business tend to do less well, as the core business must eventually decline (where are all the buggy-whip makers now?). All-out diversifiers also have a poorer success record. On average the best results go to companies who move out little by little into new but related markets and into new but related products and technologies (see the shaded area in the matrix).

Companies occasionally get startling insights when they plot the positions of their current set of products or businesses on the two axes. Sometimes the picture which emerges is surprising, sometimes a little worrying. It may raise questions: did you *plan* to be like this? Is this a satisfactory spread? What would be a more satisfactory picture?

The Growth/Share Matrix

This matrix was developed by the Boston Consulting Group (BCG) to help companies to balance their portfolios better in terms of growth businesses versus mature businesses, cash generators versus cash drains. The matrix was derived from two bases. The first was research on the Experience Curve, which linked high sales volumes with low costs and therefore high margins. The second was the Product Life Cycle, which noted that products/industries (and the companies in them) went through a life cycle with four distinct phases: Introduction and Early Growth; Rapid Growth; Maturity; and Decline. During the Rapid Growth phase industry competition was not intense but the business would need large cash investment; during the Maturity phase, competition was intense and only the most efficient would prosper. Mature businesses would need little investment and would throw off cash to feed new, growing enterprises within the company. This analysis could be applied to the portfolio of businesses in a company, or to products/services offered by a single business.

This matrix is also a simple one of two axes and four boxes. Business units or products are plotted on the two axes and are located accordingly in one of the four boxes. The boxes are referred to by their labels – Dogs, Question Marks, Stars and Cash Cows – and the model recommends a different investment approach for each.

Figure 5.3 The BCG Matrix

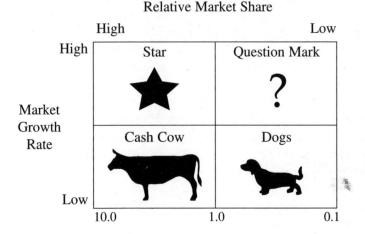

Source: Stern, C W & G Stalk Jr, *Perspectives on Strategy from the Boston Consulting Group*. Copyright © John Wiley 1988. Reproduced by permission of John Wiley & Sons Inc.

Notes

1. The vertical axis refers to Market Growth Rate; this is not to be confused with the company's growth rate.
2. The horizontal axis is Relative Market Share; this is calculated as the company's market share per cent divided by that of its largest competitor. So if the company's share is 20 per cent and the largest competitor's is 40 per cent, the company's Relative Market Share is 0.5. The axis is laid out as a log scale, and runs from 0.1 to 10.0; the centre point is 1.0 (at which the company's share and that of the largest competitor would be equal).
3. It is usual to represent each business on the matrix with a circle, and to reflect the sales turnover of each with the radius of the circle.

What the Boxes Mean

Dogs: these are businesses whose markets have gone into the low-growth phase (maturity); these businesses have a small relative market share. They therefore have a scale disadvantage at the point when the competitive intensity is highest. It will usually be difficult for them to be very profitable (unless they are operating in a defensible niche), and they are unlikely to be cash-positive. The model's advice would be to divest them.

Question Marks: these businesses (or products) are in markets which are still growing rapidly. They also have a small relative market share, but in an industry which is still growing and evolving, a small player with a competitive edge can quickly move up to a dominant position. A company may have one or more of these in its portfolio and each one requires the company to form a view: is this business/product positioned to grow rapidly and gain a dominant share, or is it stuck and will it eventually become a Dog when industry growth matures?

The answer to this question determines whether to invest more, to hold without further investment or to divest quickly. A company's Question Marks should be reviewed frequently in this light. Question Marks are heavy absorbers of cash.

Stars: stars are business units (or products) whose markets are still in high growth and who have achieved dominant relative market share (greater than 1.0). They could, of course, be displaced before the market matures, but they currently have a major advantage. It is important that they hold on to their lead, and they need to continue investing in R&D, marketing and building new facilities. If they can stay in front, they will become highly profitable. Stars may remain cash-negative for some time.

Cash Cows: when the market growth moves into its flat or mature stage, Stars become Cash Cows – businesses/products which have a dominant share of a mature market. This is a very desirable position. Cash Cows enjoy low costs and high margins through scale economies and they are hard to dislodge from their dominant positions. Since the industry is no longer growing rapidly there is little need to spend on building new facilities: R&D costs tend to reduce, and marketing intensity is usually less. The result is high profits and high cash yield.

The Concept of a Balanced Portfolio

According to the model, a company should ideally have a portfolio which contains a balance of high-growth prospects (Question Marks), high-growth dominators (Stars) and mature cash generators (Cash Cows). The following are examples of unbalanced portfolios:

Figure 5.4 Examples of Unbalanced Portfolios

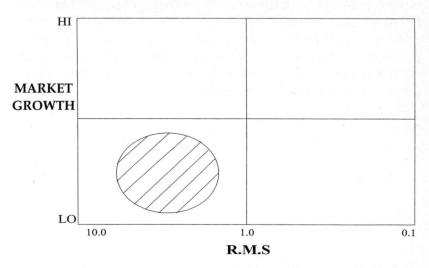

In this example the company has one big Cash Cow and nothing else. While it is awash with profits and cash right now, the question is: what of the future?

Much depends on how quickly the currently mature market sinks into decline. This is a classic problem faced by many entrepreneurial and owner-managed companies: they started in business with one really good idea in a growing market in which they achieved overall or niche dominance; now the market is mature, about to decline, and the company needs some new ideas. But is the founder receptive to new ideas?

Figure 5.5

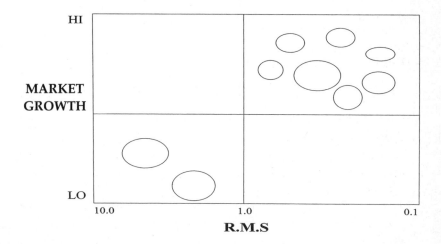

The company shown by this matrix (Figure 5.5) is having too many meetings with the bank manager. Here we have a mass of embryonic businesses or development projects being financed from a very narrow cash base. The Rolls-Royce aero-engine company looked very like this just before it collapsed in 1970: it had two engines which were selling well, and these were supporting about eight engine development projects, none of which was yet profitable.

Figure 5.6

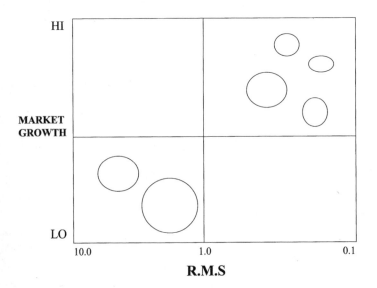

This company has a good cash base, and it has some prospects for the future, but its lack of Stars means it has no certainty of future Cash Cows to replace the current ones.

Limitations of the Model

There are a number of limitations to the BCG model:

- The model makes general prescriptions which are probably true most of the time, but may not work in a particular case.
- Market Share and Cash Generation may be important, but they make a very narrow set of criteria for judging the merits of a business unit or product.
- Not all Dogs are loss-makers; in fact, very many highly profitable businesses do not dominate their markets.

• It is often difficult to define clearly the boundaries of "the market". Most businesses operate in some segment or sector of a broad market; how that segment is defined may determine whether the business shows up as a Dog or a Cash Cow, as a Star or a Question Mark.

The Relevance of all this for you

Despite its limitations, the model does provide another way of looking at your company, and it can help to raise some interesting questions about the shape of your operations and how they are set up for the future. It is a fairly simple model, and so it can be applied without too much difficulty.

CAUTION: we have noted the model's limitations. Models and frameworks of this kind are often useful for posing important questions; they should *never* be expected to produce reliable answers.

The best advice is: do not ignore the model, but do not believe the model.

CHAPTER SIX

Developing the Strategy: Case Example

Five-year vision
Environmental review
Assessing the company situation
Priority issues and possible actions
Major strategic thrusts
Interim objectives
Action plans

"Begin with the end in mind"

Stephen Covey

"Small Opportunities are often the beginning of great enterprises"
Demosthenes (352 B.C.)

The workbook brings you through a sequence (pages 1-25) which takes Strengths and Weaknesses together with Opportunities and Threats (the SWOT analysis) and links these with Key Success Factors. The outcome is to identify a number of Priority Strategic Issues and Possible Actions. This in turn is developed into Major Strategic Thrusts, Interim Objectives and Action Plans.

What follows is a very simplified case example, designed to illustrate the sequence of thinking. It is based on a small (fictitious) road transport company operating from a base close to Dublin, Ireland.

RED LINE ROAD HAULAGE LIMITED

Red Line Road Haulage is a small Irish company engaged in general road haulage and groupage. It is based in Drogheda where it has a fairly constricted depot and it trades mostly in Ireland, with a small amount of business in the UK and Northern Ireland. It does no business into continental Europe. Its clients are in various industrial sectors and in distribution.

The company currently has eight trucks, of which four are articulated and four are rigid; it employs twenty people in total, including drivers and people at the depot. Total investment in the company is reckoned at something between £1.25 million and £1.5 million, and turnover in the year to end of last year was £2 million. Return on Investment was 8 per cent, and Return on Sales was about 6 per cent.

The owner/manager recently started attending a strategy course, and on the basis of that he has formulated a challenging future vision, as follows:

Five-Year Vision

The company aims to grow itself by Year 5 to a turnover of £6 million which means increasing by 200 per cent. It aims to do this in the computers, electronics and medical equipment industries, that is, goods in the "delicate handling" category. It aims to distinguish itself as the No. 1 quality-of-service supplier in Ireland, and to offer a service throughout Europe. It will respond to customer needs which match its growing width of competence in packaging and logistics, not limited to transport operations. It will be No. 1 in the Irish market in its niche, with 20 per cent Return on Investment and 10 per cent Return on Sales.

Environmental Review

The company looked at its environment, both the macro environment and the industry environment, and made the following notes:

Economic

High growth rates are predicted for the economy in the years ahead which will create high incomes; there is also the effect of EMU and the introduction of the Euro. It is expected that there will be more international trade within Europe and there will be growth in the high value-manufacturing sector. There will be growth in trade to and from the Continent, and over the next five years it is likely to be of the compound order of 40 per cent.

Political

It will become even easier to trade and transport across borders, although constraints and regulations on the transport industry will be more stringent. Journeys are likely to be quicker as transport infrastructure improves.

Industry Analysis

At the level of the industry, we used the Porter Five Forces Model and concluded that the forces which impacted most heavily on the company were those of **buyers** (customers) and **competitors**. Looking first of all at **buyers**, it seems likely that there will be more pressing demands for just-in-time delivery and that may mean the provision of more depots and warehousing by people in the haulage trade. Higher standards will be demanded in terms of security, safety and quality. Buyers will tend to be large, established companies with strong brands and therefore will have fairly large buying power.

In terms of **competition**, our concern here will be the presence of very large international hauliers who will trade on their reputation and their recognisable image, and who will be price competitive because of their large economies of scale. The industry in its nature is still fairly open to new entrants so there will be many small players who have either recently entered or will enter in the next few years, and they will tend to go for niche positions. We will probably see the emergence of some alliances between small players.

If we look at the customers in the industries Red Line is focusing on, it seems as if their key needs will be for quality (which includes safe and careful handling), security, dependability, responsiveness and reasonable cost.

Having looked at the external environment, we noted the following significant opportunities and threats:

Opportunities

- High growth and high margins look likely in the electronic and medical equipment sectors;
- More export and import activity;
- Better roads;
- Cheaper IT available;
- More out-sourcing and thus more component shipping.

Threats

- Growth of big carriers;
- Few unserved niche markets;
- Irish labour costs rising;
- More stringent legislation;
- Possible economic slowdown in US or Europe, which could affect multinational company MNC activity levels in the served market.

Reviewing the external environment and thinking in terms of the particular customers the company is focusing on in its target sectors, we then thought about what are the **key success factors** that any company would need to be successful in this kind of situation and we came up with the following:

1. An excellent information and tracking system;
2. Trained, flexible and committed staff, especially drivers;
3. First-class trucks and handling equipment;
4. Partnering/alliance arrangements with Euro carriers.

We decided that to achieve the levels of growth to which the company was aspiring, it would need to be perceived as outstanding in the first two of these success factors. Having analysed the external environment in relation to opportunities, threats and key success factors, we then looked at the internal company situation.

Assessing the Company Situation

The company was established in 1980 and has been profitable in most years with small losses or break-evens in the years 1984-85 and 1991-92 when trade was fairly bad. The growth over that time has been mostly self-financed and profits have been ploughed back. Current long-term loans come to £150,000 and short-term loans to £30,000.

Profitability and Growth

Return on Investment for the past five years was as follows:

Last year: 8 per cent;
Previous four years: 10 per cent; 8 per cent; 7 per cent; 9 per cent.

Recent growth has been strong. Last year the company's turnover grew by 17 per cent and in each of the previous two years it grew by 10 per cent.

Customers

Forty per cent of the business comes from four Multi-National Company (MNC) subsidiaries; 60 per cent of the business comes from twenty other companies including MNCs, indigenous manufacturers and retail. All of the customers are based in Ireland, one of them in Northern Ireland.

Reputation

The company has a solid reputation: it has good references, though not extraordinary; it is very strong on punctuality (owner/manager's values); and is considered dependable.

Premises

It has a depot and a small warehouse in Drogheda. The space around it is constricted so there is not much room for expansion and there is some ongoing friction with the neighbours. Security is provided by a contract security firm.

Fleet

The company's fleet consists of four articulated trucks, two of which are fairly new, that is to say bought in the last few years, and four rigid trucks which are smaller: one of those is new, one is fairly new and two are old.

Staff

There are twenty staff and these are the owner/manager, the night manager, two office and two maintenance people. Along with that we have fourteen drivers, of whom four are part time. The average service of these is four years and the average age is 34. There is no union. Staff are paid at about the national average for truckers and there are small bonuses for time discipline. Labour turnover is fairly low, we think, at 10 per cent, and absenteeism is at around 6 per cent. Staff relations are informal and people work quite flexibly. Recruitment is local and is carried out on a fairly informal basis, usually by recommendation or personal acquaintance.

Following our review of the company's situation, we noted its strengths and weaknesses:

Strengths

The company has a few relative strengths in its approach to this business. These few are:

- The vision, ambition and commitment of the founder;
- A sound customer reputation based on twenty years' trading;
- A strong base of business in the MNC sector;
- A record of faster-than-average growth and moderate profitability.

Weaknesses

- Small player, resource-constrained in finance and equipment;
- Little management specialism, no dedicated sales/marketing;
- Little formal system in evidence;
- Unstructured staff recruitment and training.

Priority Issues and Possible Actions

As we looked back on our lists of Opportunities, Threats, Strengths, Weaknesses and Key Success Factors, we came up with a list (in no particular order) of priorities to be addressed:

- Initially, identify/select one or two key MNC customers in the target segment;
- Approach them and sell the service to them;
- Design, monitor and manage the service for each customer;
- Find a source of long-term financial support for the growth programme;
- Establish a reliable information and tracking system quickly;
- Set up a system of staff recruitment and training, with demanding targets;
- Discover potential customers' real needs, in detail;
- Set up a programme of fleet upgrade and renewal over time;
- Specialise management support for diverse functions of marketing, systems, operations, human resource, finance;
- Set up alliance/collaborative arrangements with continental carriers or logistics companies;
- Recruit new management in key areas such as marketing/sales;
- Find a new location for expanded depot operations.

Major Strategic Thrusts

The set of priority actions identified above can be clustered or woven together so that the strategic agenda can be organised around a few central themes or thrusts. Deciding on what to group together (and how) requires judgement and creativity – we are crafting the shape and emphasis of the strategy here. We might even decide not to address all the priorities identified, but to craft a strategy which aims at only a selected part of the opportunity set.

In this example, we might reasonably decide on a strategy built on four major thrusts, each with possible subsidiary elements as indicated:

1. **Market and service creation**: recruit marketing specialist, identify target customers, do customer research, devise service package, recruit key customers, set up account management.
2. **Building the human resource**: get expert support (eventually recruit specialist), identify needs, set up recruitment criteria and system, training process, staff management and reward systems.
3. **Building physical resources and systems**: establish IT and tracking system quickly, set up fleet upgrade process, plan for new depot location, build operating linkages with partner carrier and warehousing companies.
4. **Financing the growth**: consider options, get advice, choose mix of options and acquire financing sources sufficient to drive the growth plan through a range of positive and negative future business settings. Hire expertise and/or finance specialist as the business grows.

INTERIM OBJECTIVES

1. Milestones (Progress Markers)

The company has quantified goals for Turnover, Return on Investment (RoI) and Return on Sales (RoS). It has projected progress to these goals via the following milestones:

Year	Turnover	RoI	RoS
1	£2.5m	10%	7%
2	£3.5m	15%	8%
3	£4.2m	15%	9%
4	£5.1m	18%	9%
5	£6.0m	20%	10%

2. Stepping-stones (Necessary Intermediate Events)

For each of the four major strategic thrusts, we identify a sequence of key events and processes over the plan period, consistent with achieving our Milestone targets; we then assign appropriate target dates to each event or process.

Thus, for Building Physical Resources & Systems, we might have a sequence roughly like this:

Event/Objective	Date
1. Select IT systems	Year 1, March
2. Select tracking systems	Year 1, March
3. Replace/update first of current fleet	Year 1, June
4. Locate new depot site	Year 1, September
5. Integrate IT system in place	Year 1, October
6. Start search for continental partner	Year 2, January
7. Tracking system in place, GPS-based	Year 2, January
8. Replacement of current fleet completed	Year 2, June
9. Complete move to new depot	Year 2, September
10. Set up formal linkage with continental partner	Year 2, November
11. Acquire 4 new trucks	Year 4, June
12. Acquire 4 new trucks	Year 4, January

We would construct a similar sequence of events for each of the other three major strategic thrusts.

Instead of creating lists of events and dates, we could alternatively set this out in graphic form as a project plan chart, so that the whole plan can be seen at a glance. Software packages are available to facilitate this; they can make it easy to update and modify the plan, as will frequently be necessary.

ACTION PLANS

To get the process moving, we now create a set of Action Plans for the first year – with emphasis on the first six months. This will detail the sequence of specific actions necessary to deliver each of the Steppingstone objectives described earlier.

Thus, for Objective No. 3, Replace/Upgrade 1st of Current Fleet, the following actions might be proposed:

Objective	Actions Required	By Whom	Completion Date
Replace/Upgrade 1st Lorry of Current Fleet	1. Technical specification finalised in relation to target customer needs	General Manager Maint. Head	Year 1, January 31
	2. Collect info on available suppliers & equipment options	Maint. Head	Year 1, March 1
	3. Identify preferred option & arrange financing	General Manager Maint. Head	Year 1, March 31
	4. Place order	General Manager	Year 1, March 31
	5. Train relevant staff	Maint. Head Ops. Head	Year 1, June 15
	6. Delivery & commissioning of new truck Old (rigid) truck sold off	Maint. Head General Manager	Year 1, June 30

CHAPTER SEVEN

Implementing Strategy and Managing Change

Getting a clear focus for change
Managing the change process
The importance of culture
Dealing with resistance
The key elements of successful strategic change

"The incremental approach to change is effective when what you want is more of what you've already got."

Richard Pascale

"Even if you're on the right track, you'll get run over if you just sit there."

Will Rogers

GETTING A CLEAR FOCUS FOR CHANGE

The Workbook sections on Setting Interim Objectives and Action Planning give a basis for translating your long-term intentions into tangible and short-term actions. This is a good start to the Implementation process, but it may turn out to be more complicated than that.

In Chapter 5 we introduced McKinsey's 7 S Model as a device for looking at the organisation's strengths and weaknesses. Its best use, however, is in fleshing out the agenda when we come to implement the new strategy. You may recall that the model says there are seven inter-connected facets in any organisation which must always move in the same direction; otherwise the organisation is pulling against itself and goes nowhere.

Figure 7.1 McKinsey 7 S Model

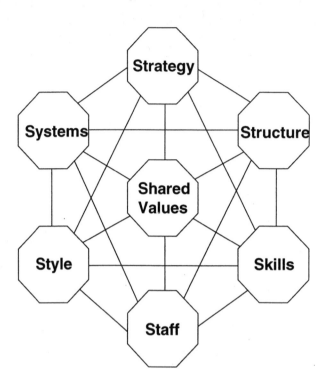

Copyright © 1980 McKinsey and Company, Inc. Used with permission.

Before we started our strategy review, the organisation was probably in balance, with the seven facets more or less aligned. If we now propose a major change in the Strategy, it will require matching changes in the organisation's Structure and Systems for a start; that much is obvious to most managers. What is perhaps less obvious is that most strategic change requires significant changes for people, their skills, how they work together, and the culture of the organisation and the workplace. These are represented by the "soft" facets – Staff, Skills, Style and Shared Values – which are often given cursory treatment by unwary managers. There is a shamefully long list of strategy implementations which have failed down the years, and a high proportion failed because the four "soft" facets were not managed actively; instead, naïve managers assumed that "all that other stuff will sort itself out". The result was that while management pulled in a new direction, the "real" organisation continued on its course and the outcome was a stalled strategy.

Therefore if we are planning a major strategy change, we need to think through what the new situation will look like in terms of each of the other facets. A useful approach is (for each facet in turn) to write down a short "snapshot" description of the position as it is now, then to write another for the end position when the strategy is achieved. This gives an effective Gap Analysis for the change programme.

Figure 7.2 Gap Analysis

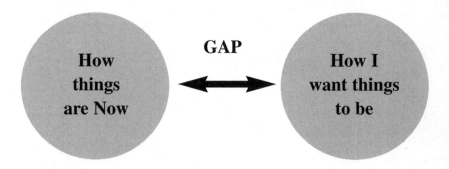

The differences between the two snapshots provide the agenda of changes you must manage explicitly in relation to that particular facet.

Focus your Efforts

Change efforts often fail because managers try to do too many things at one time; they become overwhelmed by the complexity, the sheer number of things to be done. It doesn't have to be that way. Remember Pareto's Principle: 20 per cent of the effort will deliver 80 per cent of the results, so find the key 20 per cent. How? Try breaking the objective down into the many elements necessary for its completion (see Figure 7.3 overleaf). Then estimate roughly how much each component element contributes to achieving the objective. You will usually find that just a few of the elements will deliver 80 per cent or more of the desired results; focus on these, and experience some real progress.

Figure 7.3

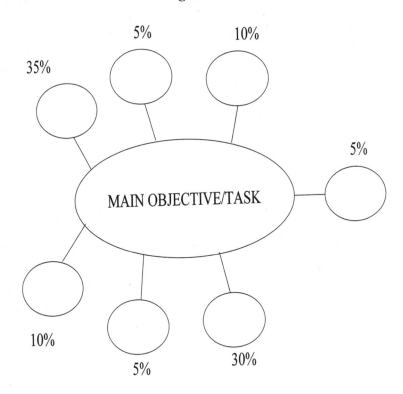

MANAGING THE CHANGE PROCESS

As we noted in Chapter 4 many industries are characterised by *punctuated equilibrium*, where periods of relative stability are interspersed with bouts of major upheaval. With each upheaval, companies typically hope they can recognise the need, make the change, bed it down and then resume a more or less balanced state. The period between upheavals is not flat calm; most companies' normal state is one of continuous tactical adjustment to small-scale changes. Therefore a company needs to develop change-competence at two levels:

1. Enough adaptable and broad-skilled people, flexible assets and resourceful management to enable it to cope with the tactical demands of continual change;
2. A system of organisation and management which can anticipate the need for **major** change, mobilise the company, execute the change quickly and maintain high performance and morale.

In this chapter we are primarily concerned with the second of these, the ability to manage major – or strategic – change. We will consider how to mobilise people in the process and how to embed the new strategy.

Kurt Lewin proposed a model which describes major change management as a three-stage process. It says that we must first **unfreeze** the present situation, then **change** to the new strategy, then **refreeze** the new approach so that change becomes the norm. These stages are also sometimes referred to as **Creating Readiness, Transition and Institutionalising.**

Figure 7.4 Lewin's Transition Model

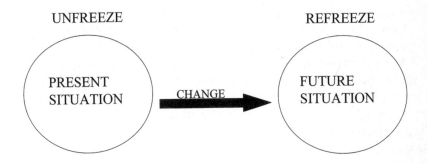

Source: Lewin, Kurt, *Field Theory in Social Science* (New York: Harper & Row) 1951.

Unfreezing/Creating Readiness is possibly the most important stage, as it is the foundation of all that follows. Many change efforts have collapsed because of the leaders' impatience to get on with the job. A manager with a compelling vision may not understand that others do not see it quite so clearly; or it may be that they see more pain than gain in it for themselves. In these circumstances, managers are often tempted by the idea that if you simply push people into a new situation, their hearts and minds will follow. Richard Beckhard created a formula which neatly summarises the elements necessary to mobilise people in major change.

Beckhard's Change Formula:

Change can happen when $D \times V \times S > P$

D = Dissatisfaction with the status quo
V = Clear vision of a desired future
S = Knowledge of the first practical steps towards the vision
P = The pain of change

Notice the multiplication signs in the formula. If one of the elements is very deficient, the impact on the change process is massive.

Sometimes it is easy to create dissatisfaction with the status quo. There may be a clear and present crisis facing the business, for example an aggressive new competitor, a change in legal regulation, a sales slump or a revolutionary technology. Under these circumstances, most people will recognise the need to move, and will look for a lead. But often the crisis is not so obvious to people. There may be a slow, long-term loss of market share, a slowing in the company's rate of innovation and a gradual loss of image in the marketplace; the company is getting into a rut, and its people at all levels are becoming less flexible, less proactive. This is a crisis indeed, but it can go unnoticed for years because its development is so gradual.

Charles Handy (1989) has written of this as the Boiled Frog phenomenon. If you pop a frog into a pan of hot water, the frog will instantly jump out; he's no fool. But if you place another frog in a pan of cold water and apply a slow heat, the frog will become sluggish and drowsy, and will eventually boil; this is because a frog's sensory apparatus is not set up to detect small incremental changes in its environment.

So if you want to make people uneasy with the status quo, you need to think about how to do it. You could share some of the information on which your own unease is based. Will it be seen as biased? Could you involve people in some additional data-gathering and discussion? Would it help to take people to visit customers, competitors, equipment suppliers or trade shows? What about an internal climate survey to give you a better sense of how people feel about the way things are going? As a positive outcome of all this discussion and consultation, you may discover new information or insights which cause you to modify and improve your original plan.

THE IMPORTANCE OF CULTURE

Any attempt at major change in an organisation is likely to collide with the culture, and in truth the hard part of organisational change is changing the culture.

CULTURE is sometimes defined as the total of the collective or shared learning of the organisation or work group. It consists of:

- VALUES and ASSUMPTIONS about *what* is important;
- BELIEFS about *how* things work, what is possible;
- BEHAVIOUR norms – "how we do things around here".

A company's culture helps to create meaning for people; it substitutes myth and beliefs for an analysis of the facts, and so it simplifies the world for its members. It supplies approved answers for how to behave in most situations.

It is mostly implicit. People are unaware of it as a fish is of water. Signs of a company's culture can be seen in the structure; in how managers behave; in what is measured and respected; in what is rewarded; in the "war stories" and the heroes who are celebrated; in rituals and taboos, symbols and ceremonies.

The culture is constantly growing and adapting to the new experiences of the organisation, but the huge accumulated burden of its history prevents any rapid change of direction. Even the present management has achieved its past successes with the established culture.

Because culture becomes relatively fixed it can inhibit the ability to see new possibilities and to adapt to change.

How can we Change the Culture?

This requires an approach on many fronts:

- Change the structure and resource allocations;
- Introduce new technology;
- Change personnel: as the saying has it "If you can't change the people, change the people";
- Make people more aware of the present culture – aspects of it which are retarding the company. There is a notion which says people must first know what *is* before they can decide what *ought* to be;
- Leaders model the new style and behaviour; senior managers in any company are the most influential shapers of culture;
- Change what is measured and rewarded. Reward innovation, risk-taking, compliance with the new culture;
- Manage the symbols: new heroes, new celebrations, new myths.

Culture cannot be changed in a day, and it cannot be changed without strong and sustained commitment to a new vision of what the organisation is to be about. Senior management must approach this with energy and enthusiasm; if you don't buy your own dream you can't sell it.

DEALING WITH RESISTANCE

You can expect some resistance to change, as people find it difficult to let go of the past. Some of the people who fear they will lose under the new situation may be right; and some of these may never come to support the change. You don't need to have everybody on board, but you do need a critical mass.

Who do you need with you? There will be some key influencers in pivotal positions who will have to be brought along. It may help to arrange people along two dimensions: Positiveness of Attitude and Energy.

Figure 7.5

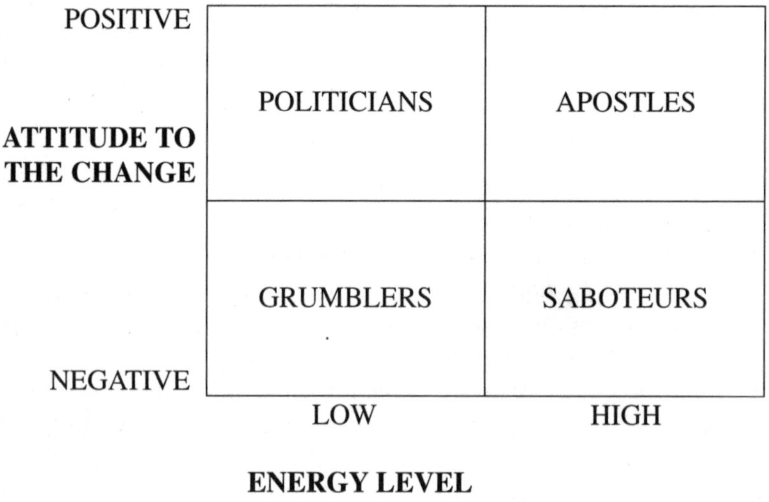

POSITIVE		
ATTITUDE TO THE CHANGE	POLITICIANS	APOSTLES
	GRUMBLERS	SABOTEURS
NEGATIVE		
	LOW	HIGH

ENERGY LEVEL

Apostles are your necessary allies in driving the change; support them, encourage them, reward them with public recognition.

Politicians will not actively promote the change, but they will express support and go along willingly. Acknowledge their support and encourage them.

Grumblers are opposed to the change, probably fearful, but are unwilling to stand out against it. Ultimately they will go along with whatever is decided elsewhere. Do not spend too much time worrying about them.

Saboteurs cannot be ignored. You may be able to convert them into Apostles (see below). Otherwise you should limit their influence; do not reward their behaviour or encourage their contribution to meetings. It is important that you are not seen to attack or punish them, as this would rally sympathy and support for them.

Handling Resistance

Why do People Resist?

- Some people expect to lose out;
- Misunderstanding, undercommunication or low trust leads people to see more harm than good in the change;
- Different assessments – people genuinely believe the change is bad for the organisation;
- Low tolerance for change – people may feel unable to learn new skills;
- Change is seen as a criticism of past decisions.

How do we Deal with it?

- Go for small commitments first and build gradually;
- Identify the prominent resisters and ask: why do they resist?
- Develop different approaches to deal with each. Be aware of the costs and benefits of each approach and in what circumstances it should be used;
- Slow the process down to give them time to build commitment.

Approaches to Converting Resisters

- **Communication and Education**: if lack of information seems to be the problem. Credibility may be an issue;
- **Participation and Involvement**: important when you need their information and ideas, and if they have the power to stop the

change. It may help to reduce fear and build commitment, but it is time-consuming;

- **Manipulation and Co-optation**: bringing them in to the process to ensure their co-operation, rather than to benefit from their contribution;
- **Explicit and Implicit Coercion**: creates resistance, and revenge will be hidden, underground. Use only as a last resort, when you have power, and speed is essential.

Force-Field Analysis

This model by Kurt Lewin (1951) is a simple and practical way to focus on what to do in overcoming resistance to change. The forces working for and against the change are shown as arrows pushing from left and right against a centreline. We first identify the forces on each side, and we then assign to each a numerical value in the range 1-10 depending on how strong we judge it to be. We then draw in an arrow of proportionate length and direction for each force. For the change to take place, the total length of the FOR arrows should exceed that of the AGAINST arrows.

For example, suppose that the particular change initiative we are working on is the introduction of team working in a group whose members have heretofore worked and been measured as autonomous individuals. Some of the forces might look like this:

POSITIVE	STRENGTH
Mutual support and synergy	5
Joint learning	6
Critical mass of ideas	4
Unity of vision, cohesion	7

NEGATIVE	
Group think	4
Measurement and rewards unclear	7
Too many meetings	6
Duplication	4
Individual initiative stifled	8

We set up the diagram with positive (from the left) and negative (from the right) arrows whose lengths represent the strength of each force. In this case, the aggregate of the negatives is greater than that of the positives. What can we do to realise the considerable benefits we know will accrue from a team-based organisation?

Figure 7.6 Lewin's Force-Field Model

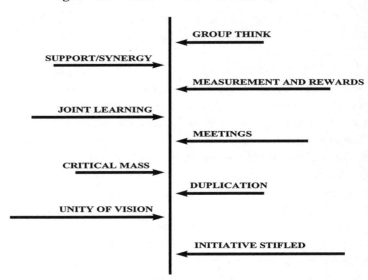

Source: Lewin, Kurt, *Field Theory in Social Science* (New York: Harper & Row) 1951.

To move the line to the right, it is recommended that attention be focused on reducing the negative forces rather than increasing the positive ones. Unilaterally increasing the forces pressing for change can have the effect of evoking an equal and opposite reaction.

THE KEY ELEMENTS OF SUCCESSFUL STRATEGIC CHANGE

Experts in this field differ in matters of detail, but there is a fair measure of concurrence about the core items. These can be summarised as follows:

- The change must be championed by the top person in the organisation, and must be led and driven by a number of top team members, not just one person.
- The need for the change must be seen at all levels of the organisation. There must be a widely shared sense that the status quo is no longer tenable.
- There must be a compelling vision and strategy. There needs to be a sense of long-term direction and purpose in the change.
- All aspects of the change should be communicated about, repeatedly and extensively, to everyone. Overcommunication beats undercommunication.
- The change should accommodate bottom-up, as well as top-down elements; so participation and local customisation should be encouraged.
- The programme should deliver some early and visible successes; this builds confidence and consolidates support for the ongoing campaign.
- The company's system of rewards and recognition must be re-aligned with the objectives of the change programme and the new strategic goals.
- The effect of not doing this is to reward resisters. One of the most popular management articles is entitled "On the folly of rewarding A while hoping for B".

References

Abell, D F, *Defining the Business: the starting point of strategic planning* (N.J.: Prentice-Hall) 1980.

Ansoff, H I, *Corporate Strategy: an analytic approach to business policy for growth and expansion* (New York: McGraw-Hill) 1965.

Hamel, G, *Leading the Revolution* (New York: Harvard Business School Press) 2000.

Hamel, G & Prahalad, C K, *Competing for the Future* (New York: Harvard Business School Press) 1994.

Hamel, G & Prahalad, C K, "Strategic Intent" *Harvard Business Review* (1989) May-June.

Handy, C B, *The Age of Unreason* (UK: Business Books) 1989.

Henderson, B, *The Product Portfolio* (Boston: The Boston Consulting Group) 1970.

Hill, C W L & Jones, G R, *Building Blocks of Competitive Advantage* (Boston: Houghton Mifflin) 1995.

Hill, C W L & Jones, G R, *Strategic Management Theory: an integrated approach* (Boston: Houghton Mifflin) 1995.

Johnson, G & Scholes, K, *Exploring Corporate Strategy* (UK: Prentice-Hall) 1995.

Levitt, T, "Marketing Myopia" *Harvard Business Review* (1975) Sept-Oct.

Lewin, K, *Field Theory in Social Science* (New York: Harper and Row) 1951.

Mintzberg, H, "Crafting Strategy" *Harvard Business Review* (1987) July-August.

Mintzberg, H, "Strategy-Making in Three Modes" *California Management Review* (1973) winter.

Porter, M E, *Competitive Advantage: creating and sustaining superior performance* (New York: The Free Press) 1985.

Porter, M E, *Competitive Strategy: techniques for analysing industries and competitors* (New York: The Free Press) 1980.

Prahalad, C K & Hamel, G, "The Core Competence of the Corporation" *Harvard Business Review* (1990) May-June.

Van der Heijden, K, *Scenarios: the art of strategic conversation* (UK: Wiley) 1996.

Index

IRISH MANAGEMENT INSTITUTE

The Irish Management Institute is a not-for-profit membership organisation at the forefront of management and organisational development in Ireland. It works with individuals and organisations to improve performance through excellence in the practice of management. The IMI has built an international reputation in the field of adult learning and through its work, contributes to Irish economic and social development. The IMI provides management training and development for more than 4500 individual managers every year. Through our conferences, regional structures and programmes, we provide a forum for our members to exchange experience, access international expertise and develop leading edge management practice.

Irish Management Institute,
National Management Centre,
Sandyford Road,
Dublin 16, Ireland.
Telephone: 353 1 207 8400
Fax: 353 1 295 5150
Email: reception@imi.ie
Website: www.imi.ie